Upcycled Fashions for Kids

31 Cute Outfits to Create from Found Treasures

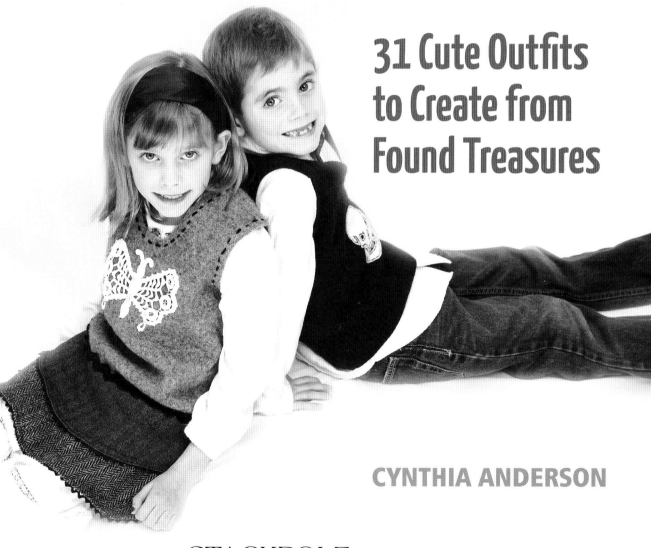

CYNTHIA ANDERSON

STACKPOLE
BOOKS

0 11557 01325 2

This book is dedicated to my future upcyclers:
Trinity, Ethan, Kira, Alexander, Christian, Isaac, and Tatum.

Published by
STACKPOLE BOOKS
5067 Ritter Road
Mechanicsburg, PA 17055
www.stackpolebooks.com

Printed in the United States of America

10 9 8 7 6 5 4 3 2 1

First edition

Photos by Cynthia Anderson and Tiffany Blackstone Photography
Cover design by Wendy A. Reynolds

Library of Congress Cataloging-in-Publication Data

Anderson, Cynthia (Seamstress)
     Upcycled fashions for kids : 31 cute outfits to create from found treasures / Cynthia Anderson.
        pages cm
     ISBN 978-0-8117-1325-2
     1. Children's clothing—Pattern design.   2. Children's clothing.   3. Clothing and dress—Remaking.   I. Title.
TT640.A53   2014
646.4'06—dc23
                                                                2014019209

Contents

CHAPTER 1

The Scoop on Upcycling

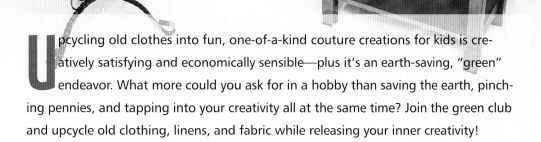

Upcycling old clothes into fun, one-of-a-kind couture creations for kids is creatively satisfying and economically sensible—plus it's an earth-saving, "green" endeavor. What more could you ask for in a hobby than saving the earth, pinching pennies, and tapping into your creativity all at the same time? Join the green club and upcycle old clothing, linens, and fabric while releasing your inner creativity!

Upcycling 101

What is Upcycling?

Upcycling is taking something of little or no value and making it into something of more value without negatively impacting the environment. It is a way to make good use of limited resources, save the energy costs and climate impact of recycling, and stretch your creativity. Upcycling old clothing is not just creating art, it is designing and producing actual wearable clothing as well. It is a way for the artist to express inner creativity in a practical, yet whimsical way.

Why Go Green?

Do you know how much clothing goes to the landfill every year? According to the EPA, eighty-five percent of unwanted clothing is discarded and accounts for more than four percent of municipal solid waste volume. The EPA Office of Solid Waste reports that Americans throw away more than sixty-eight pounds of clothing and textiles *per person per year.* In 2005 the volume of discarded clothing in the United States was eight million tons. It has continued to increase since then.

So stop throwing it away! Extend the life of out-of-style, ill-fitting clothes by refashioning them. Give your old clothes a second chance and keep them out of the landfill by redesigning them into something more practical, stylish, and usable.

Make Something from Nothing

You'll spend less and leave a smaller carbon footprint by making something of greater value out of something you either already own or can buy at the thrift store for next to nothing. Six or eight worn T-shirts cut and sewn together make a smashing new This & That Skirt (see page 34) with very little effort. A sack of lining fabric from the '50s can have a new life as an Ombre Skirt (page 73) guaranteed to turn heads. Just because the moths have feasted on a sweater doesn't mean it can't have a new life as a practical skirt, vest, or jumper (like Our Lady Upcycles, page 16). Upcycling what you already have makes more room in your budget.

Incorporate Family Memories

Upcycling allows you to incorporate bits and bobs of family heritage as tangible symbols of traditions and memories in a project. From a button off of great-grandfather's World War II uniform to pockets made from daddy's silk graduation tie or a piece of lace from mommy's wedding dress, it is so satisfying to tuck a family memento into an upcycled work of art.

Wabi Sabi

Wabi Sabi is a Japanese aesthetic that embraces the nature of the impermanent, of imperfection and the transient. It honors finding beauty in nature, and accepting that there is a natural progression of growth, decay and death. Wabi Sabi embraces that which is aged, worn, and shows the wages of time and wear. Wabi Sabi would be shopping at thrift stores and flea markets, not the shopping mall. Keep this concept in mind as you work on these upcycling projects. None will be perfect and none will last forever. Things you upcycle won't be perfectly symmetrical, they won't be permanent, they won't be costly. They *will* be ingenious, stylish, and give great personal satisfaction.

Basic Materials and Equipment

Best Sources for Upcycling Fodder

First of all, you need old or unwanted clothes to work with: old sweaters, dresses, suit coats, dress shirts, and so on. You'll also want a stock of table linens, handkerchiefs, dresser scarves, pillowcases, and other old fabric items, both to use in the projects in Chapters 7 and 8 and as sources for gorgeous old embroidery, lace trims, and fabric scraps for linings. Almost any cast-off item can be used in some way!

Your family's closets are the first best source for items to upcycle. Of course, giving unwanted or outgrown clothing to a friend or charity thrift store is another way to clear out your closet. But many items aren't suitable for this use. Set aside items that are:

- stained
- too worn
- torn or moth-eaten
- too warm or too cool for your climate
- seriously outdated

Such items will bring no value to the resale shop, and would likely just end up in the landfill anyway. But you can give them new value by making something new out of them.

After you raid your own and your family's and friends' closets for unwanted items, try the following sources for more upcycling fodder:

- thrift stores
- clothing exchanges
- resale/consignment shops
- lost and found departments
- yard sales, estate sales, tag sales, and garage sales

You'll find cheap materials to craft with as well as reduce the amount of solid waste going to landfills.

Preparing the Fabrics for Production

Always wash your found clothing and household linens before you upcycle them. Sometimes an item is so old and so fragile that it disintegrates as you wash it. While this is heartbreaking, it is better to know it can't be used *before* you have invested time and energy in transforming it into something new.

Exceptions to the wash-first rule might be centuries-old textiles or fabrics that you can see are already shredding without touching the water. These fabrics aren't a good choice for projects that will be worn regularly, but if you are making an item that will be used on one occasion—such as a christening dress, first communion dress, or flower girl dress—and then saved as an heirloom, working a piece of fragile antique textile into the project works great.

Wash cottons and linens by hand. Presoak them in a chlorine-free stain remover to get rid of as many stains as possible.

To felt wool sweaters, machine-wash them in color groups and dry them in the dryer. If you have just one sweater to felt, you can boil it in a big pot on the stove, stirring frequently and vigorously until it is felted as much as you want it. Store the felted sweaters by colors in big plastic tubs or self-closing bags.

If you like, you can dye your sweaters and fabrics to get custom colors; this is a separate art in itself. I recommend you start your dyeing experiments on smaller projects, trying different methods. Take a class or study online tutorials to learn more about dyeing fabric.

Basic Equipment

A sewing machine, nothing fancy, is necessary for this upcycling adventure. There are parts of the projects you can do by hand-sewing, but a sewing machine will serve you well for long seams. You will also need pins, thread, safety pins, an iron and ironing board, scissors, and a rotary cutter and mat for many of the projects.

Notions

Elastic

You can always use more elastic, in any width. Never pass it by if the price is right. You can also scavenge it from clothes you're upcycling: cut the elastic off worn-out or outgrown pants, skirts, and undies that still have good elastic waistbands.

Seam Binding

Never pass up a packet or two of seam binding or seam tape at a good price at a tag sale. (If it is in its original packaging and the price says fifteen cents, you have scored some fine vintage seam binding!) There are a million ways to use seam tape. Use it like ribbon or for contrasting trim. Loop the tape and tack it every few inches around a hemline to make a lovely loopy edge trim on a jacket. Rip the tape in half lengthwise to make imperfect, frayed ribbons for trimming (as seen in Degas's Little Dancer, page 65). Use stretch lace seam tape anywhere you would use a ribbon. Because of its delicate look, it is perfect to use with other more solid ribbons, as on Silver Linings. Single-fold and double-fold bias trim comes in many colors and widths. It can be used to bind the raw edge of just about any fabric. Be sure to factor in the weight of the fabric when using a binding.

Buttons

A recycler can never have too many buttons. They are so versatile. They can be used to embellish a bodice or cover a moth hole. Use them as monster eyes, skeleton teeth, centers of flowers—the sky's the limit! Sort out the shank-back buttons from the flat buttons with holes. Shank-back buttons also make great jewelry. Then sort the buttons by colors and store them in one of those fish tackle storage boxes.

Rickrack

While rickrack is still being produced today, there is nothing so colorful as the vintage rickrack from back in the day. It is guaranteed to show up at estate, tag, and yard sales. Take it home and use it up! What could be prettier than a little edge of colorful rickrack peeping out past a hemline or the edge of a bodice (seen on Bow Peep, page 97). Don't scrimp on the rickrack.

Ribbons

Can an upcycler have too many ribbons? Impossible. Save the ribbons or cloth tape from every single package you ever receive and store them in plastic bags by color. When working on a purple project, pull out your purple ribbon stash and keep it handy. Use it for bows, for straps, for belts, or for flowers. The greater the variety of textures and shades you add to a project, the more it comes to life. Don't even think of putting a piece of ribbon in the trash—upcycle it!

Vintage Notions

Never pass a garage or yard sale without checking for sewing notions. Be a vintage notions scavenger. Every household has them and few shoppers need more. Bias tape, lace hem tape, rickrack, zippers—they can all make splendid embellishments for a green project. Use it up. Enjoy it. Don't hoard it!

Tulle

Rolls of tulle are a staple for upcycling clothes for little girls. Collect them in all colors, especially when you find them for fifty percent off or at a garage sale. A tulle flounce can lengthen something too short or jazz up something too mundane. Check the remnant rack for remnants of tulle in colors you love. Often a little snippet of tulle can be the perfect embellishment for a little girl's dream dress.

Making Embellishments

The projects in this book use many different cloth flowers and other trimmings. Here are directions for making some favorites—but there are many possibilities. Look online for more tutorials and inspiration for other creative embellishments.

Fabric Roses

You can make a rose from just about any fabric. Learning to make them gives the recycler a great sense of empowerment. To make them you need:

- Circle of fabric, felt, or tulle for the backing, 2 in. (5 cm) in diameter
- A strip of fabric, 1 to 1½ in. (2.5 to 3.8 cm) wide and 12 to 14 in. (30.4 to 35.6 cm) long

Fold your strip of fabric in half or thirds. Place the end in the center of the base circle and begin wrapping and folding the strip around the circle, sewing it down as you go. Stitch down about ¾ in. (1.9 cm) of the strip, then fold the strip and stitch another 1 to 1½ in. (2.5 to 3.8 cm). Continue stitching and folding until you have a rose that pleases you. The sizes of materials given here will yield a rose about 2 in. (5 cm) in diameter; to make a bigger rose, start with a larger circle and a longer and wider strip of fabric.

These flowers are used on the Ivory Wood Sprite sash and tiara (page 76).

Round Silky Flowers

These flowers are easy to make. You will need:

- Silky synthetic fabric
- A pearl button
- A candle and matches
- Tweezers

Start by cutting an odd number of circles in descending sizes from your fabric. For example, for a three-petal flower, you could cut a 2½ in. (6.4 cm) circle, a 2 in. (5 cm) circle, and a 1½ in. (3.8 cm) circle.

Light the candle and use it to alter the petals. Using tweezers, hold a petal wrong side up and heat the top side over the flame. Be careful not to start a fire or burn yourself! The heat will curl the edges of the flower. For a shabbier look, you can actually singe the edges.

Once the petals are all heat curled or singed, stack them in size order and sew them together by stitching the button to the center of the stack, going through all layers of fabric.

You can make these flowers in any size. Make them as dense as you want by adding more petals in the stack; just make sure each petal is a different size from the next.

These flowers lie flat and offer a more tailored look to your project. Natural fabrics like cotton and linen will not curl up on the edges like synthetic fabrics, so this is a place to use your synthetic silky fabrics.

You can see one of these flowers on the bodice of the Violet Wood Sprite (page 41).

Scrap Dragons

These far-out flowers are fun to make, especially if you like a more spontaneous, less controlled look. To make one you will need:

- Scraps of fabric in several shades of a color group
- 3 in. (8 cm) circle of felt in similar color
- Sew-on pin back

Gather scraps of fabric in a wide range of shades of one color. Silky lining fabric recycled from old clothing is a perfect fabric to use for these flowers. This makes ready-made loops for your flowers. You can also mix in a little velvet and linen, but the silky fabrics are the easiest to use. Rip, don't cut, the fabrics into strips about 1½ to 2½ in. (3.8 to 6.4 cm) wide and 18 to 22 in. (46 to 56 cm) long.

The linings of jacket sleeves and pant legs work especially well for these flowers; you can leave the side seams intact and cut the sleeve or pant leg lining in bands 1½ to 2½ in. (3.8 to 6.4 cm) wide, like calamari or giant rubber bands.

Run a basting stitch down one long edge of each strip or band and pull the thread to gather it slightly. The gathered strip should be about half as long as it originally was.

Starting at the outside edge of the circle, begin sewing one of the strips or bands to the felt using a zigzag stitch.

As one strip is sewn down, pick up another of different fabric and continue sewing in a spiral or concentric circles.

As you get near the center, it will be more difficult to manage but you can do it! Leave the very center vacant and put a button in it later or tack a pompom or tuft of one of the fabrics in the center.

You can use the flower as is and sew a pin back on it or you can go for the gold and make it shaggy. To make it shaggy, use small sharp scissors and cut each row of ruffles from the raw edge to just short of the center. Pull a little on each raw edge as you cut the petals so they will be nice and hairy.

See one of these superstars on Lacy Lucy (page 62).

Frankenstein Flowers (Silk Flower Remix)

These Frankenstein flowers are easy-peasy to make. All you need to make them is:

- Assorted silk flowers
- Buttons for centers
- Sew-on pin back

Deconstruct a variety of silk flowers. Make new flowers by selecting three sizes of deconstructed flower blossoms and stacking them together for an entirely new species. Choose a button for the center of each flower and sew the button to the new flower to tack it together. Sew a pin back on each flower or sew them to the project you are creating.

These flowers also work as buttonhole covers. Just make a cut in the center of the flower and then sew it to the garment with the slit over the buttonhole. When you button the item, the flower will get the button as its center. See these flowers on Daddy's Little Firecracker (page 52) and Je T'aime, Paris (page 56).

Shaggy Lining Roses

These lovely flowers are easy to make and are a great way to recycle the lining of a jacket sleeve or pant leg. You will need:

- A small circle of felt for the flower back
- Some 1½ to 2½ in. (3.8 to 6.4 cm) wide bands of sleeve or pant leg lining, cut into loops
- Pin back (optional)

Cut a sleeve or pant leg lining into bands, leaving the side seams intact. Run a basting stitch along one side of the band and then pull the thread to gather it slightly. The gathered band will be much smaller in circumference than it was originally.

Sew the widest band down to the outside border of the circle. Sew several more gathered bands, working from the outside of the circle to the center. Make sure you sew some lining in the exact center of the circle so that it is all filled in. Now pull threads from the unsewn raw edge of each of the strips of fabric until the roses are as shaggy as you would like. Tack the roses directly onto the project or sew on a pin back if you want to use them as accessory pins. See three of these roses on Pierrot (page 12).

Lollipop Flowers

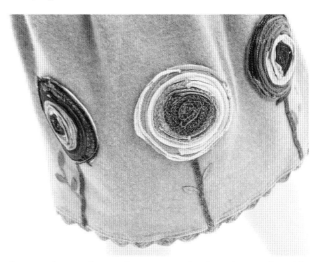

These cuties are fun and easy to make, but they make a big design statement. You will need:

- ¼ to ⅓ in. (6 to 8 mm) wide strips of recycled 100% wool fabric in a variety of lengths
- Circle of felt for the base
- Green wool fabric or felt for stems and leaves

Begin by cutting your felt circle the size you want your flower to be. Sew the strips of wool fabric to the flower in a spiral, starting in the center with the darkest strip. Keep adding new colors and stitching in a circle until the strips cover your felt circle. Place the flower on your garment and pin in place. Pin the stem in place and add a couple of leaves. Once your flower is where you want it, sew it in place by hand. See three of these on the Lollipop Flower Skirt (page 14).

Tulle Roses

These ethereal beauties are easy to make and lend a big wow factor to your project. Tulle is available (relatively cheaply) at craft stores in a variety of colors. You will need:

• A roll of 6 in. (15 cm) wide tulle

For each rose, cut a 6 in. (15 cm) square of tulle, then fold that square into a 3 in. (8 cm) square. This will form the base of your tulle rose. Cut a strip of tulle about 18 in. (46 cm) long for each rose you want to make. Fold the strip of tulle in half or thirds widthwise and place the end of the strip right in the center of the square. Begin stitching the tulle down in a circle, folding the tulle over every couple of inches to build a lovely folded circular rose. See one of these on the back of the 52 Pickup dress (page 59).

Tulle Tufts

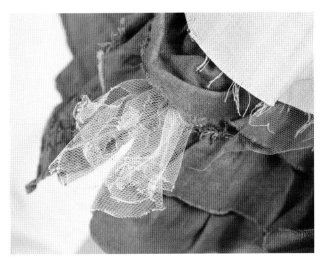

Tulle tufts are simple to make and are an easy way to add depth and interest to a project. They can be made from a roll of tulle or from tulle remnants. They serve as little grace notes or accents and bring a design to life. For a single tuft you will need:

• A small remnant of tulle or a strip of tulle from a 6 in. (15 cm) wide roll
• A candle and matches
• Tweezers

Cut the tulle into squares about 3 to 6 in. (8 to 15 cm) wide on each side. Singe the edges of the squares using tweezers and a candle. Once the edges are singed, pinch the center of each square and tack the pinch on the sewing machine. This makes a little tuft of tulle to tuck between ruffles on a skirt or anywhere you need a little tulle exclamation point. See these on the skirt of Silver Linings (page 79).

Ribbon Roses

Ribbon roses are made just like the tulle roses. You need:

• A 6 in. (15 cm) square of tulle for base of flower
• 2 colors of ribbon—one for the rose and a green for the leaves

Fold the tulle square in fourths to get a 3 in. (8 cm) square. Cut a piece of the ribbon for the rose 12 to 18 in. (30 to 46 cm) long. Place the end of the ribbon in the center of the tulle square and sew it down, going around in a circle and folding the ribbon often. Fold a 2 in. (5 cm) length of green ribbon to form a point, overlap the cut edges, and tack them under the outside petals of the rose. See these flowers all around the neck on Degas's Little Dancer (page 65).

Acanthus Leaves

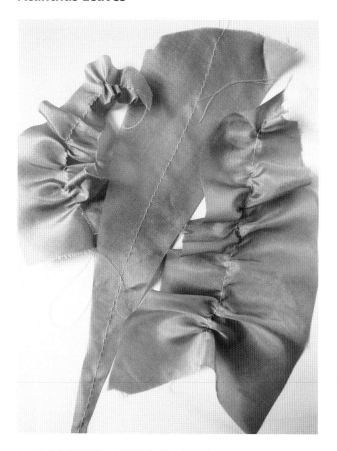

These elongated triangles can serve as foliage for the various flowers on your creations. They are very easy to make from scraps left over from past projects. All you need are long triangular scraps. Sew a line of basting stitches lengthwise down the center of the wedge. Draw the basting stitches up and voila, you have a lovely architectural acanthus leaf-like piece of foliage for your flowers. See these on the skirts of Violet Wood Sprite (page 41), Ivory Wood Sprite (page 76), and Silver Linings (page 79).

Shabby Chic Tulle

Tulle straight off the roll can be too new and pretty looking when paired with recycled clothing. It often needs a little touch of shabby chic. To achieve this more vintage look cut your tulle in pieces about 2 to 3 feet (60 to 90 cm) long. Don't measure, just estimate. Once you have cut about two dozen tulle strips, it's time to rough them up a little. Light a freestanding candle. Hold a tulle strip in both hands and move the edges of the tulle along the flame of the candle to singe them. Don't burn your fingers! Use tweezers when you can to hold the tulle and avoid burning your fingers.

Many of the projects in this book that use tulle suggest that you prepare it in this way. You can see shabby chic tulle strips on Degas's Little Dancer (page 65).

CHAPTER 2

Upcycling Sweaters

In this chapter, we will explore the joys of upcycling discarded sweaters and sweater-vests of all varieties—whether wool, cashmere, moth-eaten, or shrunken. You'll get ideas and tips for making orphaned rejects into fanciful, playful, and easy-to-make dresses, jumpers, sweaters, and skirts. From Pierrot to the Littlest Angel and everything in between, these projects are designed to be easy and quick, and make a bold and light-hearted statement for little or no moola.

Pierrot

You cannot walk into a toy store in France without seeing that beloved old clown Pierrot. Remember that nursery lullaby *Au Clair de la Lune* that addresses *"mon ami Pierrot"*? If you have ever sung that sweet song to your child, pay tribute to the memory by upcycling one of daddy's sweaters into a perfect little Pierrot party frock for your sweet little Clair de Lune.

Materials

- 100% wool ivory man's sweater with raglan sleeves
- Strip of antique lace 2 to 3 in. (5 to 6.4 cm) wide and about 2½ times as long as the circumference of the sweater's neckline
- Bands of black lining from jacket arms and pant legs
- Roll of 6 in. (15 cm) ivory tulle
- Chalk

Preparations

First, felt the sweater using the method of your choice (see page 3).

Sewing

Lay out the felted sweater and lay an A-line skirt pattern or an A-line-shaped piece of clothing that fits your child over it. Pin the pattern so that the top of the A-line meets the armpit seam of the sweater and the pattern angles out to the bottom of the side seam. Use the chalk to trace along the edge of the pattern for the new side seams of the sweater. Draw a line for cutting the sleeves off, leaving a little cap sleeve behind, starting from the raglan seam line and going outward to form the cap sleeve; when you are happy with the line, cut along it. Turn the sweater wrong side out and sew the side seams along the chalk line you've drawn from the arm hole to the hemline. Press the seams open and turn the dress right side out. Leave the sweater's neckline just as it is.

Embellishment

Choose a piece of beautiful creamy lace about two and a half times longer than the neckline measurement from your stash and run a basting line down one edge. Sew the two ends of the lace together and place it around the neckline. Pull the basting threads to gather the lace until it fits the neckline perfectly. Pin the lace in place, then sew it.

To make a tutu for the skirt, sit down at the sewing machine with the roll of ivory tulle and the dress. Start sewing the tulle to the right side of the bottom edge of the sweater ribbing. As you sew, push tucks of tulle under the presser foot to gather the tulle as you go. After you have sewn one gathered row of tulle around the very bottom of the sweater, start another row just above, again adding tucks as you sew. Finish the tutu by stitching a third row of tulle just above the first two rows. Your tutu should be very perky now.

Make three giant black shaggy roses, following the directions on page 8. Sew the roses to the front of the dress.

Styling

- This dress needs tights or leggings in ivory, black, or a combination of the two. Black and white stripes, a lace pattern, or polka dots would also be perfect. An ivory turtleneck is perfect under this warm and charming dress.
- Add a soft black knit beanie in a tip of the hat to Pierrot.

Tips

- Make one more giant shaggy rose and sew it on a headband or knit hat to top off your creation.
- Save the sweater sleeves for another project.
- If you have any stains or moth holes on the front of the sweater, camouflage them with a shaggy rose.

Lollipop Flower Skirt

Soft as cashmere and sweet as sugar—this skirt has it all! This is a simple and practical project that will expand a girl's cool-weather wardrobe and give her an outfit she's always excited to wear. Any pretty colored sweater that has a flaw above the height of the arm holes is a perfect candidate. It just takes one straight cut from armpit to armpit and you are almost there!

Materials

- Felted cashmere sweater
- ³⁄₈ in. (1 cm) bias tape
- Elastic for waistband and safety pin
- 3 pieces of felt for the flowers, about 3 to 4 in.
  (8 to 10 cm) square
- Strips of ¼ in. (6 mm) wide wool strips to form
  the face of the flowers and stems
- Chenille rickrack for hem edge

Preparations

Choose a pretty cashmere sweater and felt it using the method of your choice. Make sure that the felted sweater, when measured from the armpit to the hem, is long enough to make a skirt for your little girl. Draw a chalk line on the sweater from one armpit to the other on the front and on the back. Following the chalk line, cut off the lower section of the sweater. (Set the top section of the sweater aside to use on another project. With the addition of a lovely skirt and some decorations over any flaws, it could become a new dress for Sweet Pea.)

Sewing

To make a casing for the elastic waistband, pin your bias tape to the top edge of the right side of the new skirt. Sew along the top edge of the bias tape, then open up the seam, folding the bias tape to the inside of the skirt, and press. Pin the lower edge of the bias tape to the wrong side of the skirt, then sew it down, leaving an opening to insert the elastic through. Fasten a safety pin to the end of the elastic and thread it through the casing. Try it on Sweet Pea and adjust the elastic to fit just right. Overlap the two ends of the elastic and sew them together, then stitch the opening in the casing closed.

Embellishment

Let the fun begin! Cut three 3 to 4 in. (8 to 10 cm) circles from different colored felt. Sort through your ¼ in. (6 mm) wide wool strips and pull out three piles of strips—one for each lollipop flower. Make three flowers in different colors, following the directions on page 8 for making lollipop flowers.

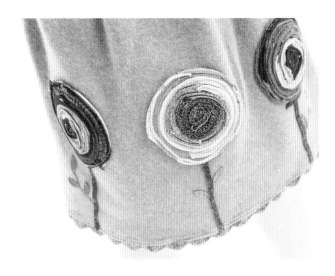

Styling

- T-shirt of your choice and a pair of tights or leggings with school shoes make this a warm and hardworking choice for cooler climates.

Tips

- Sister skirts are easy to make if you have two pastel sweaters to upcycle.
- These skirts are just as cute in dark colors as they are in pastels.

Our Lady Upcycles

Color blocking, bling, cashmere—what more could a girl want? Beautiful cashmere sweaters can be had at the resale shops for very little money. Sometimes they may have a small moth hole or snag in them but there are plenty of creative ways around a little snag or hole. That is what buttons and patches and trim are for!

The inspiration for this jumper was a beautiful sequined patch of Our Lady of Guadalupe which was a souvenir of a special vacation. The patch was so colorful and sparkly, it cried out for a colorful and simple companion. Three yummy-colored, sliced and diced, recycled cashmere sweaters go together quickly for a pretty simple project that has a whole lot of curb appeal.

Keep it simple. Three colors, three textures—one big bling!

Materials

- 3 colorful cashmere or cashmere-like sweaters
- Our Lady of Guadalupe sequined patch
- Pair of colorful socks

Preparations

Felt the cashmere sweaters using the method of your choice. If you choose not to felt them, at least wash them in hot water and dry them in the dryer to make them smaller and denser.

Lay out the prepared sweaters and decide which will be the bodice section, which will be the middle section and which will be the bottom band. Let your sweaters help you decide how this tricolor creation will go together. For this project, the turquoise cashmere sweater seemed perfect for the bodice. It had a large cowl neck and long sleeves that could easily be cut out. The center orange section came from the sleeve of a large woman's cardigan. The magenta cashmere skirt section was the lower part of a woman's vest that had a large hole in upper section. That hole made the decision to make the lower part of the vest into the skirt of the new dress.

Measure your little girl to determine how long you want the jumper to be. Lay out your three sweaters to decide the proportions you want for the colors in the dress. Once you know that, draw a horizontal chalk line around the bodice to indicate your stitching line. Next draw two horizontal lines on the center section—one for the seam with the bodice and the other for the skirt seam. Finally, draw a horizontal line around the sweater you wish to use as the skirt. Be sure to use the already finished bottom edge of the sweater to serve as the hem of the dress. The sections you select in this process will determine the total length of the finished dress. You may want to lay a dress that fits your child beside the new three-section design to confirm that the length and proportion look right.

Cut out these sections of your dress, leaving a one-inch seam allowance along each seam. Zigzag stitch along the raw edges of each piece.

Sewing

Lay down the middle section next to the bodice section and make sure they fit together, leaving a slight flare at the bottom of the middle section. Carefully pin the bodice section to the mid-section, then sew them together with right sides together. Open the seam and press.

Pin the skirt section to the bottom of the middle section and sew them together in the same way. Press the seam.

Carefully cut off the cowl collar and sleeves from the bodice sweater, following the lines where they are sewn to the main part of the sweater. Roll under a ¼ in. (6 mm) seam around each opening formed, then roll it under once more and pin it in place. Blind stitch these hems.

Embellishment

Ice this colorful cake by choosing a sequined patch or other decorative item to serve as the key feature. Pin it on the front of the dress, then hand-stitch it in place.

Make pockets from two mismatched hand-knit socks. (This pair had holes in the heels, so were a perfect candidate for upcycling.) Harvest the top part of the socks by machine stitching around each sock leg just below where you want to cut it. The top finished edge of the sock will make the top of the pocket. Cut each sock top in half (first stitching along where you plan to cut to keep the fabric from unraveling). Take one half of each sock and turn under ¼ in. (6 mm) of the three raw edges and press. Place them on the jumper and pin them in place. Blind stitch the pockets to the jumper.

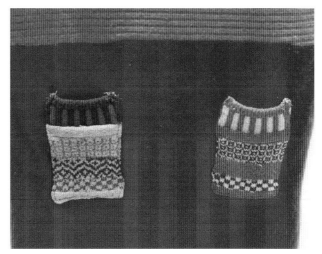

Styling

• This jumper is perfect with a black turtleneck and a pair of black tights or leggings.

Tips

• Start collecting colorful cashmere sweaters now; you can always do something with them, and more options will help you get three that play well together.
• Search your box of vacation souvenirs for a patch or appliqué that might serve as the centerpiece for a jumper.

Mr. Monster

Cast-off or accidentally felted sweaters make a quick and easy way to dress a guy in a warm sweater and an imaginative hug. Find your sweater candidate, then brainstorm with your little guy about what he wants on the sweater. Does he love pirates? Monsters? Robots? This little boy wanted a green monster sweater to wear to scare his colleagues and that wish was pretty easy to make come true.

Materials

- Green wool sweater (adult size)
- Red, white, and black felt scraps
- 4 black buttons
- Ivory rickrack

Preparations

Felt the sweater using your preferred method. Ask your little monster to draw a monster face or draw one yourself and submit it for his approval. You only need eyes, mouth, and nose to make your face recognizable. Make it unique!

Once you have drawn the face you like, cut out the components from scrap felt. Use ivory rickrack for the teeth and black buttons for eyeballs and nose holes.

Try the sweater on your little monster and see if he likes it and if it fits as is, or if the sleeves need to be shorter. Another option is to cut the sleeves out completely, making the sweater into a vest. Because your sweater is tightly felted you will not need to hem where you have shortened or removed the sleeves.

Embellishment

Pin, then sew down the whites of the monster's eyes first. Next, sew on his button eyeballs, then his eyebrows. Place his nostrils where they belong and stitch the two smaller buttons in place. Place the ivory rickrack on the red rectangular mouth. Fold over and press the red top and bottom of the mouth in place so that only half of the rickrack shows and it looks like teeth. Pin, then sew to hold the teeth in. Place the mouth on the face and stitch it in place.

You can hand-sew all these elements or use the sewing machine. It's your call.

Styling

- A vintage pair of grey wool flannel shorts and a white shirt with the tail hanging out would look mighty fine on a good-looking young buck. Add some black knee socks and some boots and the man is ready for special-occasion fun—or at least a photo op!
- With a pair of jeans, this sweater dresses down nicely for playtime, too.

Tips

- Big-box craft stores sell rectangular sheets of felt in many colors for less than a dollar each. If you don't have a stash of felt scraps, you can buy your monster features for less than a buck.
- If you choose to make your sweater into a vest, be sure to save the two sleeves to use in another project.

Dem Bones

There are few things little boys like as much as trucks, motorcycles, and skulls! This project is such an easy and satisfying one. With some shrunken or felted wool sweaters and a scrap or two of felt you can make a little man happy and warm at the same time.

Bones 1

Materials

- Black 100% cashmere sweater vest
- Piece of ivory felt
- Sheet of paper
- Pencil
- Black permanent felt-tipped marker
- 3 small pearl or bone buttons

Preparations

Felt the cashmere sweater vest using the method of your choice. Find a drawing of a skull in a coloring book or on the Internet and modify it, if desired, until you have a design that pleases you. Sketch it onto a piece of white paper. Go over the pencil drawing with the permanent marker. Place the sheet of ivory felt over the drawing. You should be able to faintly see the black marker areas through the ivory felt. Use the pencil to trace the outline onto the felt sheet. Stitch around the black spaces on the ivory felt two or three times with black thread, so that the outline of the skull is clearly stitched on the felt.

Sewing

Take the sheet of felt and place it in the center of the front of the vest. Pin it in place. Stitch it to the front of the vest using the black topstitching as your guide. This one was sewn on the sewing machine, but you could do the stitching by hand if you prefer.

Once the ivory skull is sewn to the black vest front, cut out the holes in the skull—the nose and eye sockets and the space between the skull and the jawbone—to expose the black of the vest underneath. Snip carefully with sharp scissors and make sure not to cut the vest.

Embellishment

Sew the three tiny pearl or bone buttons to the vest in the space between the skull and the jawbone. Those will form the skeleton's spooky teeth.

Styling

- Jeans and a nice white shirt will take a guy out on the town in this luxurious upcycled vest. Add a silk bow tie to kick it up another notch.

Tips

- Choose 3 different tiny pearl or bone buttons for Bones's teeth. They are spookier if they are not all alike.

Bones 2

Materials

- White 100% wool man's cardigan
- Piece of black felt
- Sheet of paper
- Pencil

Preparations

Felt the wool sweater using the method of your choice. Find a drawing of a skull in a coloring book or on the Internet and modify it, if desired. Sketch the skull onto a piece of paper. Lay the pencil drawing of the skull over the sheet of black felt and pin it in place. Cut out the skull from the felt.

Sewing

Pin the felt skull to the sweater, then machine stitch it in place with white thread. Be sure to stitch around the eye and nose sockets and the jawbone so that the skull is firmly attached to the sweater. You could leave the threads long where you have sewn it down for a spookier look.

Styling

- A newsboy hat, a chambray shirt, boots, some tweedy knickerbockers with suspenders, and the man is ready for his GQ cover shot!

Tips

- If the sleeves of the sweater you have felted are too long for your little guy, just cut them off. Tightly felted wool sweaters won't unravel.
- Make knickerbockers out of a pair of dress slacks that are too short but still fit the kid.

Bones 3

Materials

- Yellow 100% wool crewneck sweater
- Stewart plaid wool scarf
- Piece of ivory felt
- Sheet of paper
- Pencil
- Double sided iron-on interfacing

Preparations

Felt the wool sweater and muffler using the method of your choice. Find a drawing of a skull and crossbones in a coloring book or on the Internet. Sketch your version of it onto a piece of paper, then cut it out. Pin these pattern pieces onto the plaid fabric and trace, then cut out the plaid skull and crossbones. Iron both pieces to the rough side of the interfacing, then cut around them. Cut out holes for the eyes, nose, and mouth in the skull.

Trace around the plaid skull and crossbones on the piece of ivory felt. Cut out the ivory felt, leaving a ⅓ in. (8 mm) margin around the plaid skull and crossbones. Place the plaid skull and crossbones on the ivory pieces and iron in place. Finally, iron the skull and crossbones to another piece of interfacing and cut around them.

Sewing

Place the skull and crossbones on the center front of your felted wool sweater and iron them in place. Use the sewing machine to stitch around the edges of both pieces to attach them more firmly to the sweater. Stitch around the eye and nose sockets and the mouth as well.

Styling

- Khaki slacks or jeans, a white, striped, or plaid shirt, some loafers or boots, and the little man is ready for a big event like a holiday dinner.

Tips

- Moth-eaten plaid scarves are perfect candidates to become the skull and crossbones.

Heidi's Après Ski Skirt

Fair Isle sweaters have an eternal appeal. The moths must have agreed with that statement, as they ate heartily from this one (as well as the other three solid-color sweaters used in this little skirt). While the larger parts of these sweaters went to make jumpers and dresses, the sleeves were all that was needed to make this sassy little skirt. Doesn't it look like something Heidi would wear by the fire in the ski lodge with a ski sweater and some faux fur-lined boots? This is a pretty simple project which can be made the easy way— or (a little more difficult) with pockets and trim.

Materials

- Four 100% wool sweater sleeves, felted
- $7/8$ in. (2.2 cm) bias tape for waistband
- Elastic
- Chalk
- Measuring stick
- Beaded drapery trim
- Scrap of cotton packaging tape for bow
- String of bells

Preparations

Using the method of your choice, felt four 100% wool sweaters. For this project, I used two patterned sweaters—Fair Isle and striped—and two in solid colors. Turn the prepared sweaters wrong side out and find the spot where a sleeve seam meets the side bodice seam of the sweater. Using sharp scissors, carefully cut the sleeve from the sweater, using the "gutter" of the seam between the shoulder and sleeve as your guide. Next, cut the sleeve seam open, following the sleeve seam "gutter." Open out the sleeve and press it flat. Repeat with one sleeve from each of the other sweaters.

Sewing

Lay the four sleeves out with the cuffs as the top of the skirt and the raw ends as the bottom edge of the skirt. Decide on the order you want for the panels, then sew the four side seams and press.

Measuring down from the waistband, mark the length you want the skirt to be with chalk. Allow $1/2$ to 1 in. (1.3 to 2.5 cm) for a hem if you are going to do a folded hem with trim as shown here.

Embellishment

The two pockets are made from the extra parts of two sleeves that were cut off when evening out the bottom edge of the skirt. The curved edges will serve as the bottom edges of the pockets. Run a basting stitch along the long straight edge of each piece, then pull the basting to gather the top of the pocket and stitch along that line to hold the gathers in place. Pin the two pockets to the side panels of the skirt and sew around the sides and bottom.

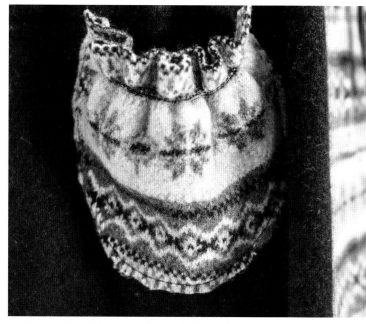

Turn under a $1/2$ to 1 in. (1.3 to 2.5 cm) hem around the bottom edge of the skirt and press. Pin the beaded hem trim in place, then sew it and the hem in place. The skirt shown here uses two different remnants of trim—use what you have!

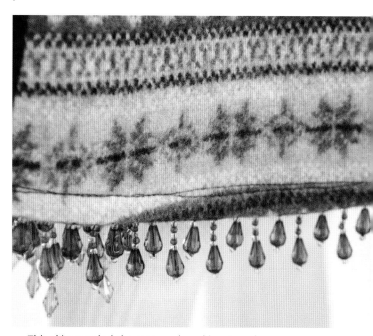

This skirt needed the tatty red packing tape bow and the string of bells to cap it off. The bow and bells are safety pinned to the skirt so they can be removed for the wash.

Styling

• Jeans-style leggings or tights, some sheepskin boots, and a big red or ivory sweater would make the perfect après ski outfit for your little Heidi.

Tips

• The shoulder ends of the two patterned sweaters become the two pockets of this skirt.

The Littlest Angel

Did someone read *The Littlest Angel* to you when you were a child? My great aunt read it to me many years ago, and I pored over the illustrations showing the Littlest Angel all suited up to bring special gifts to the newborn baby. This pearl-encrusted sweater I found in a thrift shop immediately brought that dormant image back to my mind. A nice hot bath, a few feathers, tulle, and a rummage through grandmother's lace and ribbon treasure box brought this Littlest Angel sweater to life. Can't you picture a little angel in your family attired in a dress, wings, and halo like this? Somebody grab the camera!

Materials

- Pearl-trimmed angora/wool cardigan sweater
- 2 lengths of crocheted lace attached to fabric (I used trim from a dresser scarf)
- Roll of ivory tulle
- Decorative ribbon
- Ivory ribbon
- 2 shoulder pads
- Ivory satin scraps to cover the shoulder pads (a half-yard remnant is more than enough)
- Pattern for A-line jumper
- Marking pencil or chalk
- Fabric glue or hot glue gun
- White marabou feather boa
- White feathers
- Freezer paper
- Lightweight wire
- Silver and gold tinsel
- Speckled egg, feather, and rock

Preparations

Felt the sweater using the method of your choice. Find a lovely piece of vintage crochet, tatting or lace to use as the flounce of the skirt. You will need a piece of lace trim that is slightly longer than the lower edge of the sweater (after felting). Leave about an inch of the original item (in this case, a dresser scarf) attached to your upcycled trim to use to sew the lace to the sweater. Press the raw edge of the fabric under.

Sew the ivory tulle to the underside of the trim just above where the lace is attached to the linen. Take pin tucks as you stitch the tulle to the trim, gathering the tulle; use a pointed object such as a seam ripper to push a little tuck into the tulle as you stitch. Attach a second tulle ruffle in the same way.

Stitch a basting line on the top edge of the linen the lace is attached to. Stitch a second line of basting just above the stitching line where you attached the tulle. This will help you gather in the lace to perfectly fit the hem of the skirt. Set the lace/tulle panels aside.

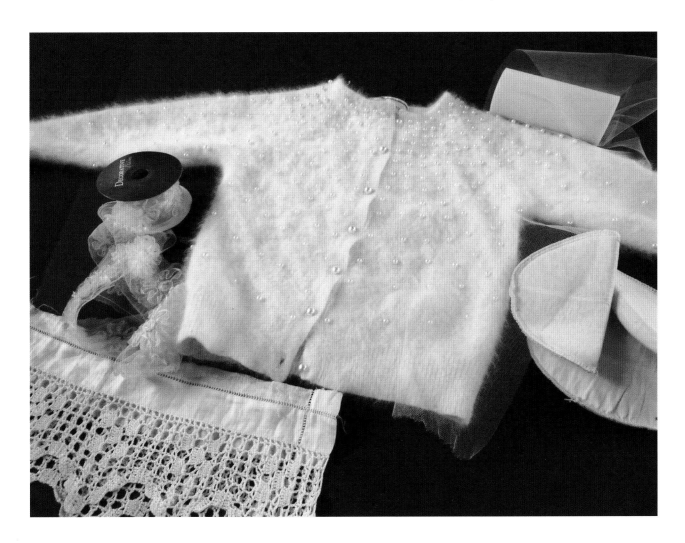

Sewing

Lay the A-line pattern down on the front of the dress. Keep the neckline of the sweater just as it is. Use the pattern to show you where to taper in the side seams from under the arm to the ribbing at the bottom. Use a marking pencil or chalk to mark that side seam line. Also mark a line to cut a small cap sleeve.

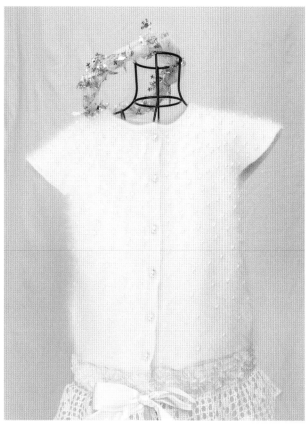

Using very sharp scissors, cut along the lines you marked on the front of the sweater. Turn the sweater over and mark the back side seams and the back of the cap sleeve in the same way, then cut.

Turn the sweater wrong side out and sew both side seams. Press the seams open and turn the dress right side out.

Embellishment

Pin the two lace/tulle ruffles to the bottom edge of the dress, starting at the center back of the sweater. The cardigan I used for this project had a ribbed band at the bottom edge that tapered back in. That wasn't the shape I wanted for this dress, so I attached the trim right where the sweater joined the ribbing, before it tapered back in. Pull the basting threads so that each of the two ruffles fits from center back to center front. Pin the ruffles in place. Sew them to the dress along the top where the panel starts and at the bottom, just above the lace and tulle. Sew a decorative ribbon over the top of the linen band to cover it.

Wings

Make a wing pattern by laying two large white or ivory shoulder pads side by side on a piece of freezer paper and drawing the shape of a pair of wings freehand around them, making them larger than the actual size of the shoulder pads (you are making a slipcover for the shoulder pads). Leave 1½ in. (3.8 cm) of space between the two wings. Extend the shape of the outside edges of the pattern to make the wings longer on the outer edges and shorter on the inner edges.

Cut out the pattern, lay it on the satin, and trace around it. Cut the pattern out from the satin twice—once for the front and once for the back of the wings. Place the pieces with wrong sides together and sew around the edge, leaving an opening to turn the wing cover right side out. Turn the pieces right side out and insert the pads. Sew a channel down the center between the two shoulder pad wings, then stitch the opening closed. Sew two pieces of ivory ribbon to the center of the wings, one at the top and one at the bottom, to use to tie the wings to the dress.

Using fabric glue or a hot glue gun, glue the marabou feather boa in horizontal strips across the wings, starting a few inches from the bottom edge and moving up. Once one side is covered, turn the wings over and repeat on the other side. Glue individual feathers along the bottom edge of the wings so that the feathers extend past the satin body of the wings. Sew a ribbon onto the center back of the dress near the neckline and another a few inches lower. Use the two ribbons to tie the wings to the dress.

Halo

Wind the wire into a circle the size of your angel's head. Wrap ivory or white scraps of fabric and ribbon around the circle, then wrap tulle around the halo. Finish by tying decorative tinsel and ribbons around the halo.

Lace Bag

The little angel needs a lace bag to carry her treasures in. Fold a piece of lace in half and sew up the side and bottom seams. Sew a ribbon handle onto the bag. Place a bird's egg, a tiny feather, and a little rock in the bag, along with a tag, written by the angel and reading "To: Baby Jesus; From: The Littlest Angel."

Styling

• This little angel will need some tights in ivory or black and some Mary Jane shoes, ballet slippers, or boots.
• A long-sleeved ivory turtleneck will keep the angel warm on a winter's day.

Tips

• Start looking right now for the perfect white angora sweater. They are rarer than baby bird teeth!
• The sleeves from this sweater will be perfect in a skirt later.

CHAPTER 3

Upcycling T-Shirts

Every household has some stained, too small, or worn-out old T-shirts. You can take a pile of cast-off T-shirts and make darling kid couture from these pieces you thought were useless and headed to the landfill. Sassy skirts, ombre dresses, and fanciful wood sprites—your recycled T-shirts have never looked better.

This & That Skirt

What fun it can be to throw together some old favorite T-shirts and stir them up into a mash-up of a funky new skirt. This skirt is like a crazy quilt in some ways; you are using what you have, and the rules are few and far between.

This wraparound skirt is composed of five panels, but your skirt could have more or fewer panels, as long as it fits your little sweetie. One of the panels in this skirt is made from two different T-shirts—the top half of the panel is one shirt and the bottom half is another. You can mix and match your panels any way you like in order to use additional T-shirts.

Pick one of your T-shirts for this project with a design on it to feature; you will appliqué it over a couple of the panels of the skirt. It should have a great graphic on it that will make the other colors in the skirt pop.

Sew this project with a happy heart! Choose by colors, choose by memories, choose by sports—just choose a selection of T-shirts that pleases you, and your This & That skirt will put itself together before your very eyes. This skirt reminds me of the essence of Wabi Sabi—it won't last forever, it won't be perfect, and it might not be symmetrical, but it will be pretty darn cute on some little girl!

Materials

- Discarded parts of 7 or 8 different T-shirts
- 1 in. (2.5 cm) wide horizontal strips of various T-shirts
- Rotary cutter, ruler, and mat
- Large paper bag

Preparation

Choose the shirts you want to work with, then wash, dry, and press them lightly so that you have a smooth surface to cut. You will be cutting with the rotary cutter on the mat so you want wrinkle-free, smooth T-shirts to cut apart.

Make a pattern for the skirt panel from the paper bag. The length of the pattern should be however long you want your skirt to be. Make it wide enough that five panels sewn together will be enough to go around your kid's waist and overlap about 12 to 16 in. (30 to 41 cm).

Cut some strips about 1 in. (2.5 cm) wide from several different colorful T-shirts. Cut the hems off the bottoms of two T-shirts in colors that complement the skirt and save these strips for the waistband.

Sewing

Use the pattern you created to cut out the panels for your skirt. Lay out the panels in the order you want to use them. Go to the machine and sew them together in order, overlapping them slightly. Press the seams and try on the skirt to make sure it fits and overlaps appropriately.

To make a simple waistband, you will use the bottom hems of two T-shirts. This gives you more body in your waistband than using a strip from the middle of a shirt.

Take one of the T-shirt bottom bands you cut earlier and sew it to the top edge of the skirt. Move the band as you sew so that it meanders along the top of the skirt.

Next sew down the second bottom band, meandering about above, below, and over the first band. Once the waistband is sewn in place, topstitch over it in a fanciful way to add a bit of embellishment.

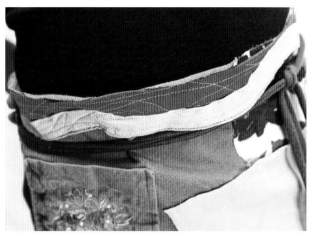

Reinforce the side edges of the skirt by first stretching then topstitching some 1 in. (2.5 cm) strips of T-shirt down both side edges of the skirt. Do the same at the bottom of the skirt. This will add color, reinforce the end panels, add body to the skirt, and provide a more finished look.

To make the ties for the skirt, take the other 1 in. (2.5 cm) strips you cut and pull them with your hands to stretch them out. Sew down two of the strips at one end of the waist and another pair at the other end. These will be the ties to tie the skirt around the child's waist.

Now add the feature panel. Pin it in place in the spot you want it, then sew it down.

Styling

- One of the joys of this skirt is that it goes with everything! A simple solid-colored T-shirt or white shirt with a collar and the girl is styled to go.
- Black or white tights and T-shirt highlight the Wabi Sabi essence of this piece.

Tips

- Save favorite T-shirts from team sports, charity runs, and family reunions. Even if they are outgrown or stained, they can be harvested for this project.
- This project has no relationship with perfection. Give it up for random!

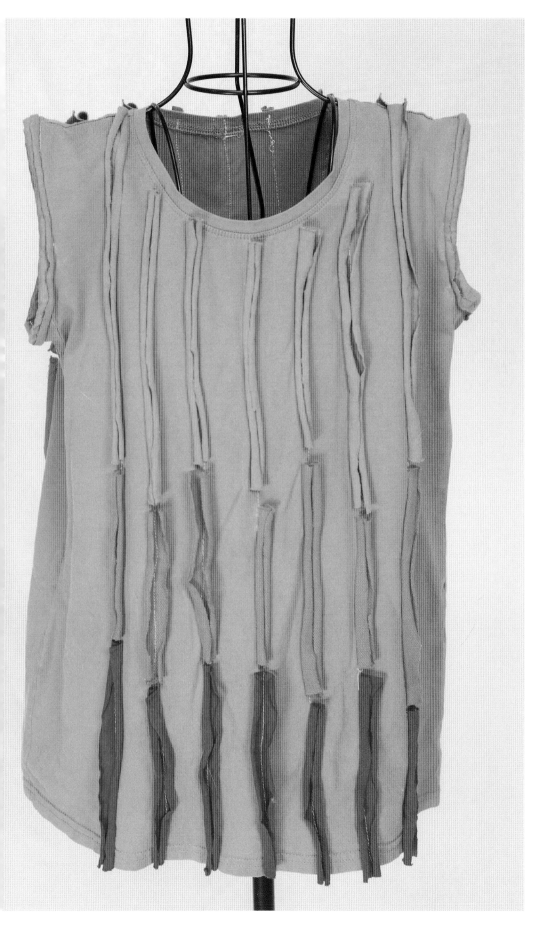

Sunset Shift

This simple project produces such a pretty ombre effect with very little effort. The hot pink T-shirt came to life when the three shades of orange T-shirt strips were sewn on. Picture your little seashell sifting sand at the seashore at sunset in this spiffy shift!

Materials

- A short-sleeved woman's T-shirt
- Cotton T-shirts in three shades of one color
- A-line shift or dress pattern
- Chalk

Preparations

Wash, dry, and iron the base T-shirt so that you will have a smooth surface to work on.

Choose three T-shirts that are three shades of a color that harmonizes with the base T-shirt and cut horizontal strips 1 in. (2.5 cm) wide from them.

Lay the pattern on the T-shirt and mark the lines to cut with chalk. Cut along the lines, leaving the neckline of the T-shirt just as it is.

Embellishment

Draw a chalk line down the center front of the dress. Take a strip of the lightest color T-shirt and, starting at the top, begin to sew it down along this line. When you get about a third of the way down, cut the strip off. Take up a strip in the second color and sew it down along the middle third of the center line. Finish with a strip in the darkest color. Next, sew down another set of three strips, in the same order, an inch or two (2.5 to 5 cm) to the left of the center line. Add another column of strips to the right of the center. You won't need chalk lines for this part; just place the strips parallel to the center line. Finish the front by adding lines four and five to either side of the first three columns.

Now turn the dress over and embellish the back in the same way.

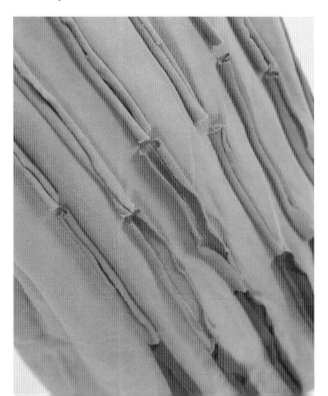

Finishing

Sew up the side seams of the dress. To finish the armholes, select a strip of the lightest color of your 3 ombre colors. Starting at the underarm seam, fold the strip in half lengthwise and pin it around the raw edge of the armhole. Either hand-stitch it in place with a pretty color of yarn or machine stitch in place.

Styling

- Sandals and a bracelet or two will finish off this simple summer look.

Tips

- Make sister dresses from their favorite colors and have the girls pose for a rainbow picture.

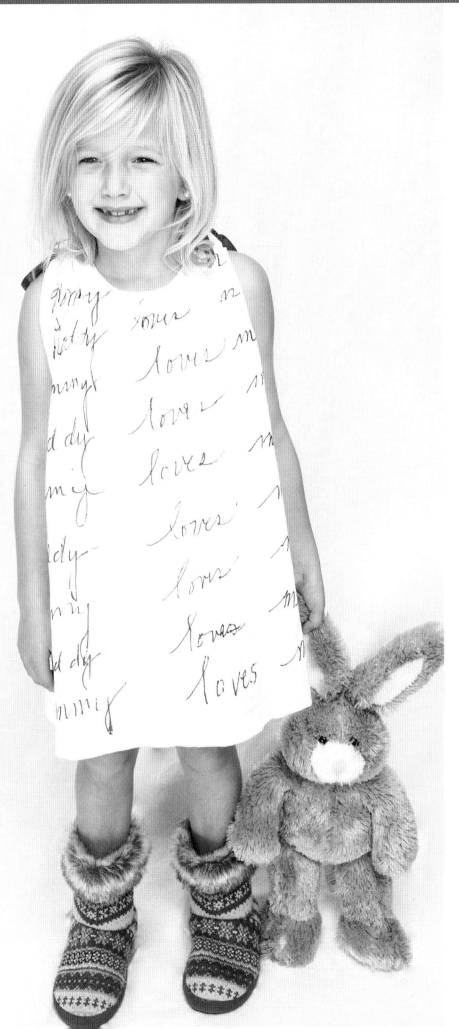

Nightie Night

All you need is love—and an old white T-shirt! What could give your little girl sweeter dreams than to be wrapped in the love of her mommy and daddy all night long? This project involves very little sewing; in fact, it doesn't even require a sewing machine if you don't have one.

Materials

- Soft white T-shirt
- Wax paper or freezer paper
- Black permanent fabric marker, medium tip
- Hot pink rayon hem binding

Preparation

Wash, dry, and press the T-shirt before beginning the embellishment. You want the surface to be smooth so that you can write easily on it.

Sewing and Embellishment

Cut the sleeves off of the T-shirt but leave about 1 in. (2.5 cm) of sleeve to turn under. Turn under ½ in. (1.3 cm) of fabric around each armhole and press, then turn under another ½ in. (1.3 cm) and pin in place. Hand-stitch the hem around the sleeve opening.

It is time to write your message on the shirt. Insert freezer paper between the front and back of the shirt so that the marker doesn't bleed through to the other side. Practice writing your message on a piece of newspaper first to work out the spacing. When you're ready, start at the neckline and write the message across the shirt. Continue, line after line, until you fill the shirt. Turn the shirt over and repeat on the back.

Make two rows of basting stitches across each of the shoulder seams. Pull the threads to gather the shoulders. Tie the hot pink hem tape in a bow around each shoulder.

Styling

- Wear this with a hug and a kiss and a good bedtime story.

Tips

- Can't sew at all? No problem! Skip the sleeve hems and the shoulder gathers. Just cut the sleeves out of the T-shirt, write on it with a permanent fabric marker and tie ribbons on the shoulders, and you have a nightie full of love.
- Write anything you want on the shirt. "Happy birthday," "Grammy loves you," "Sleep Tight," "Now I lay me down to sleep"—your call!

Violet Wood Sprite

Who would have dreamed that such a gorgeous gossamer violet wood sprite frock could be conjured up out of one of daddy's old golf shirts? The T-shirt was a formerly white freebie from a tournament and had become a sallow grayish color over the years. As I looked at the old shirt, some bits of upcycled ribbons, and a bottle of dye, I began to hatch a plan. In a blaze of outside-the-box-thinking, I sewed this project together and embellished it with nothing but scraps. Who wouldn't enjoy some imaginative play in a dress that cost nothing but brings out the best in a girl's vivid imaginary world? Picture countless summer hours spent in a sylvan glen as the little wood sprite chases dragonflies and sings enchanting tunes in this ethereal violet creation . . .

Materials

- Man's cotton golf shirt
- Dye of your choice suitable for use on cotton and other plant fibers
- Tulle
- Scraps of ivory or white fabric made of plant fiber—silk, cotton, linen, etc.
- Recycled ribbons and buttons
- Lightweight wire for tiara

Preparations

Wash and dry the T-shirt, then cut off the sleeves and collar. Leave about 1 in. (2.5 cm) of each sleeve so that you will have some fabric to roll under to finish the sleeve edge.

Tear the white and ivory scraps into strips about 2 in. (5 cm) wide for ruffles. Use wedge-shaped scraps for trim and make some of the scraps into roses for embellishing the dress. Run basting stitches down one long edge of each strip and pull the threads to ruffle the strips. Run basting stitches down the centers of the wedge-shaped pieces to make ruching to place above the highest row of ruffles to camouflage the raw top edge.

Sewing

To take in the neckline of the shirt to fit the sprite, make darts or a box pleat in the center back neck of the shirt. Roll under a hem and stitch around sleeve and neck holes.

Sew the ruffles you have made onto the skirt, starting just above the hemline. Don't pin, just start about an inch (2.5 cm) above the skirt hem and start sewing, going slightly uphill as you sew the ruffle down. When your ruffle runs out, pick up another strip and keep stitching. Continue adding ruffles in an upward spiral until you have about three or four rows.

Next, dye the dress and all the fabric scraps for trim that you think you might use. Follow the manufacturer's directions for whatever dye you're using. A commercial store-bought dye is the easy way to dye your project. If you like experimenting and you are open to surprises, try using a natural dye method (look for instructions on the Internet). Be sure to pretreat the fabric and set the dye as directed in whatever instructions you are using.

Embellishment

Make a variety of roses for the dress using tulle, ribbon, knit fabric, and woven cloth from your stash of dyed scraps. Also prepare some Frankenstein flowers, singed green tulle leaves, and tulle tufts. (See pages 6–10 for directions for making roses and other flowers.)

Rip some pieces from your scraps to use as a background on which to nestle your flowers. Pin the background fabrics in place around the neckline, camouflaging the button placket and the logo, if the shirt has one. Pin a little more background fabric on the front of the skirt just above the top ruffle on the front of the dress. Tack down the fabric flowers and other embellishments you have made around the neckline, along the ruffles, and on top of the logo, buttons, and any stains.

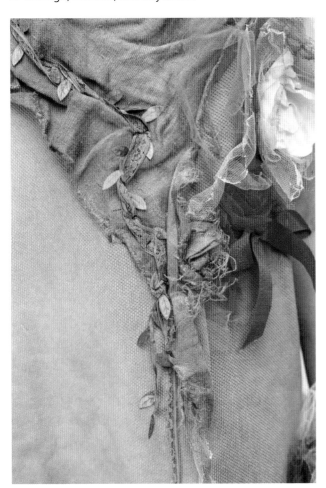

Tiara

Twist the wire into a ring. Wrap the ring in dyed fabric scraps and tulle, then embellish it with bits and bobs of ribbons, singed tulle, and fabric roses.

Styling

• This type of dress is perfect for a flower girl in an eco-green wedding. Nothing new here—it is all recycled. A nosegay or basket of flowers, her tiara, some whimsical slippers, and the girl is good to go.

• For less formal events, a black T-shirt and black tights make the girl ready to twirl to Tchaikovsky's *Waltz of the Flowers.*

Tips

• This dress is perfect for photo ops, flower girls, birthday parties, and the dress-up box.

• You can find tutorials and more information about natural dyeing on the Internet.

• Rip the fabric for ruffles for nicely frayed edges.

• Leave symmetry behind.

• Leave perfection behind.

CHAPTER 4

Upcycling Daddy's Duds

Daddy's shirts, slacks, and jackets make fantastic fodder for kids' fashions. This chapter shows you how to upgrade components from dad's cast-off wardrobe into fashion-forward designs. From wool jumpers made from daddy's sport coats and slacks, to frilly, flowery little dresses for daughter dear, everything you need to know to start upcycling daddy's duds is included in this chapter.

Sleeveless in Seattle

Remember snuggling up to your daddy and feeling that nice tweedy wooly feeling as you buried your face in his sport coat? What a great memory! Why not make that same memory for your little girl using daddy's discarded sport coats?

Materials

- 100% wool sweater
- 3 sleeves, one from each of 3 different wool tweed jackets
- Scraps of 2 more sleeves for the underskirt
- Assorted wool gabardine scraps (wool gabardine pant legs work great)
- Wool scraps for 2 different pockets
- Wool yarn and large needle
- Bodice pattern
- Chalk
- Seam ripper
- Lace scraps
- Large button
- Two 36 in. (91 cm) strips of brown grosgrain ribbon, ⅝ in. (1.6 cm) wide

Preparation

Felt the sweater and the jacket sleeves using the method of your choice. Using a seam ripper, cut the lining out of the jacket sleeves and reserve it for other projects. Press the sweater and the jacket sleeves so they are nice and smooth.

Bodice

Lay your bodice pattern on the sweater and draw a chalk line to use for cutting. Be sure to leave plenty of extra length at the bottom of the bodice, just in case you need it. Cut out the bodice and sew the side seams. (If you are lucky, the shrunken sweater will fit perfectly without having to change the side seams.)

Sewing

Choose three tweedy jacket sleeves and decide what order you want them to appear in. Pin the three sleeves together and make sure they are at least as big around as the bodice. Sew the side seams between the three sleeves. Leave the cuffs of the sleeves, which are now the top edge of the skirt, just as they are, buttons and all. Baste the skirt to the bodice, with the cuffs of the sleeves on the outside and the bodice on the inside, then machine stitch them together.

Fold the two strips of ribbon in half and mark the centers. Pin each of the ribbons to the sides of the jumper, about ¾ in. (1.9 cm) from the top of the skirt. Stitch the center 4 in. (10 cm) of each ribbon to the skirt. Put the dress on the little girl and then tie the two brown ribbon sashes into bows on either side of the jumper. They will cinch the jumper in to fit the little girl nicely.

Embellishment

Pockets

Cut two square pockets from two different tweedy scraps. Turn down the top edge of each pocket to the wrong side and press. Turn under ⅜ in. (1 cm) along the side edges of the pockets and press. Place the pockets where you want them on the front of the skirt and pin them in place. Using wool yarn, sew the pockets to the jumper with a running stitch that will show. Use a different color of yarn on each pocket.

Hemline

Leave the hemline of the skirt as a raw edge. The jacket shoulders will form a fun, wavy hemline. Use four more wool jacket scraps to fill in the hemline where the waves go up.

One of the scraps should be a partial cuff of a jacket. Pin the cuff, with its buttons still on it, in the center front hem curve. The other three pieces can be cut from the curvy shoulder ends of other jacket sleeves. Pin these three shoulder ends in place at the other high wave spots on the hem. Sew them in place with the sewing machine, about ½ in. (1.3 cm) from the raw edge of the main skirt pieces.

Make sure this raw edge is appropriately frayed. Using the wool yarn, add decorative hand-stitching over the machine stitching around the bottom of the hem.

Next find some tacky old brown lace to trim the center front cuff piece. Spray starch on the lace and crush it up, then press it with a very cool iron in order to make the lace look way less than perfect.

Bodice Neckline and Armholes

Cut some 2 in. (5 cm) wide bias tape from some recycled wool gabardine jackets or slacks. Leaving the edges raw, pin the bias tape around each armhole and around the neckline. Use two colors, a different one for each armhole and both on the neckline. Hand-stitch these bias strips in place using wool yarn. Attach a nice big vintage button on the neckline.

Styling

- In chilly weather, a creamy turtleneck, brown, navy or black cotton tights, and some nice brown lace-up boots would be perfect for this ensemble.
- Vintage bloomers might look extra cool under this little tribute to daddy.
- A headband with a big dark grosgrain bow would top it off nicely.

Tips

- Never say no to someone who wants to give you an old wool sport coat or wool gabardine slacks. They can be used for many cool projects.
- You might need to melt the brown lace trim over a votive candle a little to make it look extra old and ragged. Don't burn yourself!

Flutterfly

A dresser scarf with needlework butterflies on each end started it all. The crocheted butterfly was begging to be featured on a nice neutral gray background for a precious little girl. Upcycling the wool sweater from daddy (and what daddy doesn't have an old gray sweater to donate to the cause?) and the wool for the flounces from two of his tweedy wool jackets makes this totally "green" project a charmer. Finding the cuffs of a pair of antique pantaloons at an estate sale prompted the addition of the warm and comfy old-fashioned bloomers. Can't you picture a little Edwardian girl twirling a hoop in the park in this ensemble of dropped-waist dress and pantaloons?

Materials

- Gray wool sweater, felted
- 2 sleeves from 2 different tweedy wool jackets
- Seam ripper
- Embroidered/crocheted/lace butterfly from dresser scarf or other old household linens
- Old sheet or scrap muslin for pantaloons
- Medium-sized black rickrack
- Giant black chenille rickrack
- Dropped-waist jumper pattern
- Pants pattern
- Ruffles from a pair of vintage pantaloons
- Elastic, ¼ in. (6 mm) wide
- Safety pin

Bodice

Felt one gray wool sweater, then cut out a bodice from it using a pattern for a dropped-waist dress or jumper. The pattern used here was Butterick B4842 but any similar pattern would work. Lay the bodice front pattern on the felted sweater and draw a chalk line around it. Use the sweater's natural shoulder line; don't cut the front and back of the sweater apart at the shoulders. Be sure to chalk in the sleeve opening. Carefully cut out the front of the bodice, then turn the carcass of the sweater over and draw a chalk line around the bodice back pattern, again leaving the shoulders connected. Carefully cut out the back of the jumper.

Sew up the side seams. This sweater was so well felted that I could overlap the front of the sweater over the back by about ¼ in. (6 mm) and simply topstitch the two layers together. If your sweater is not as well felted, pin the right sides together and sew up the side seams. Press the side seams open.

Skirt

Wash two men's wool jackets in hot water and dry them in a hot dryer to felt them as much as possible. Using a seam ripper, rip out a sleeve from each of the jackets. Use the seam ripper to remove the lining from the sleeves, but leave the cuff edge of the jacket just as it is so that it can be used later for another project (such as for filling in the gaps in the Sleeveless in Seattle dress, page 46). Lay the front and back patterns for the first flounce on the first sleeve and cut them out (if you do not have a large enough section of fabric to cut the first flounce on the fold, cut each piece out in two halves and sew them together). Cut the second tier of flounces (front and back) from the second jacket sleeve. Sew the front pieces to the back pieces. Press the seams open and then press under ¼ in. (6 mm) along the bottom edge of each tier. Place the rickrack under the bottom edge of each flounce and topstitch it in place. Baste the top flounce to the bottom flounce to form the skirt.

Pin, then sew the skirt to the bodice and press the seam.

Embellishment

Carefully remove your butterfly applique from its original source. Lay it on the bodice, making sure to center it, and pin it in place. Hand-stitch it to the jumper with thread the same color as the butterfly.

Pantaloons

From a soft, old bed sheet or muslin remnants, cut out the pattern pieces for a pair of knee-length pants to fit your child. Modify the pattern you use to fit the size of the vintage flounces that you plan to use. Sew the pantaloons together and make a waistband casing. Thread the elastic through the casing, adjust it to fit your child, and sew the ends together, then sew up the opening in the casing.

Pin the vintage flounces to the bottom edge of the pantaloons and sew in place. Sew or pin bows to the front center of the top edge of each flounce.

Styling

- In cool weather, wear black tights or leggings under the pantaloons.
- A white blouse with a Peter Pan collar works perfectly under the jumper.
- A giant black silk hair bow and a nice pair of boots will cap off this Edwardian charmer.

Tips

- Make easy pantaloons by sewing ruffles onto a pair of knee-length leggings.

Daddy's Little Firecracker

Daddy's fine cotton dress shirts are soft, colorful, and expensive. Why toss them when they have a stain or snag? Recycle them into a fetching, three-tiered dress for your little firecracker. She can wear this on several patriotic occasions and any occasion honoring our veterans.

Materials

- 3 cotton dress shirts of different colors
- 3 colors of rickrack
- Assorted silk flowers
- Assorted ribbons for bows
- 3 yd. (2.7 m) grosgrain ribbon, 1½ in. (3.8 cm) wide
- 2 pin backs
- Package of single-fold bias tape

Preparations

Cut the shirts as shown in the illustration into dresses with straight top bodice edges, curved armholes, and flared skirts. Leave the bottom edge of each shirt intact. Cut the three dresses all the same size side to side, but make the middle layer dress 3 in. (8 cm) shorter than the bottom layer dress, and the top layer dress 6 in. (15 cm) shorter than the bottom layer.

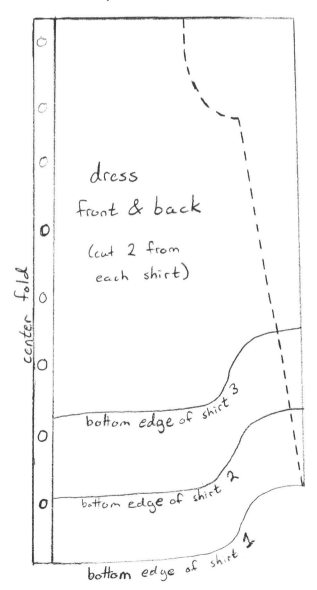

center fold

dress
front & back

(cut 2 from each shirt)

bottom edge of shirt 3

bottom edge of shirt 2

bottom edge of shirt 1

Cut out two double-thick bands 3 by 10 in. (8 by 25 cm) from the back yokes of two of the shirts for the front and back yokes of the dress.

Sewing

Sew up the side seams of each of the dresses and press the seams open. Sew rickrack under the hem of each dress, letting it peek out from under the shirt hem.

Next, stack all three dresses one inside the next, with the shortest dress on the outside and the longest on the inside. Sew the dresses together across the top edge of the bodice in the front and back. Run two basting lines across the top edge on both sides so that you can gather the neckline in a little to fit your little flag waver.

Sew the three dresses together around the armholes. Sew single-fold bias tape to the outside of the top dress along both underarms (but not across the top of the bodice). Press the tape under and sew it in place to the inside of the dress.

Take the double bands for the yokes, fold under and press a ½ in. (1.3 cm) seam allowance on all four sides of these pieces. Fold them in half horizontally to form two self-lining yokes and press again. Open up the pieces and sew the seam allowance of the one piece to the top edge of the front of the dress and the other to the top edge of the back. Fold them along the line you pressed, pin them to the top edge of the dress on the inside, then sew them in place.

Cut two 8 in. (20 cm) shoulder straps from the grosgrain ribbon. Fold the ends under and press. Sew the two straps to the insides of the yokes on both sides at the proper length for your child. (You will add the big bows later.)

Now balloon the bottom of the shirts. Gather up three or four tiny horizontal tucks in the side seam and tack them down using the sewing machine. Next, make a set of tucks in the center of the back of the dress. Last of all, gather up some tucks in the center, on either side of the button placket.

Embellishment

This is where the fun begins on this project!

Flowers

These are Frankenstein flowers—they are made from the parts of other flowers. Choose some flowers from your stash that have the colors of your shirts in them. Pull them apart and save the little plastic bits for other projects. Make a hybrid flower by stacking three flower parts on top of one another, with the largest on the bottom and the smallest on the top. Use scissors to carefully cut two short straight lines in the center of the flower to form a cross. Slip the flower over a button and tack in place using the sewing machine. Repeat for each of the front buttons.

Bows

Rip some small strips from the leftover parts of the shirts you have used. The strips can be 6 to 10 in. (15 to 25 cm) long and about ⅝ in. (1.6 cm) wide. Highlight the raw edges by shredding them a little. Tie a little knot in the middle of each streamer. Cut some small lengths of ribbons and tie them in bows.

Pin the streamers and bows to every spot where you tucked the skirt. Rearrange them until you are pleased with the design, then sew them in place, sewing through the central knot of each embellishment.

Make two large grosgrain bows for the front bodice of the dress. Once you have them tied the way you like them, sew them each onto a pin back. This way, when you wash the dress, you can take the two front shoulder bows off and keep them tied perfectly.

Styling

- For summertime, tie grosgrain ribbon bows on a pair of flip flops. A sparkler is the only other accessory needed!
- For cold-weather wear, add a long-sleeved T-shirt and red shoes.

Tips

- You can find many different patterns for recycling a man's shirt into a girl's dress online.
- The center of each flower down the front is the actual shirt button that was left in place.
- Isn't this a perfect frock for 4th of July, Bastille Day, Memorial Day, or Labor Day (or Veteran's Day, with a shirt underneath)?

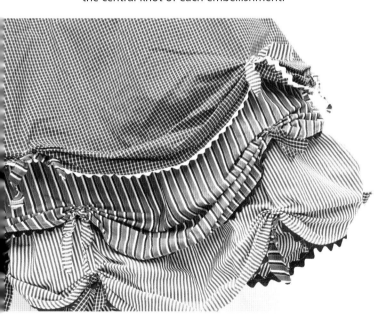

CHAPTER 5

Upcycling Mommy's Apparel

Just because a piece of clothing is no longer in style doesn't mean it's time to throw it out. Women's outdated couture can become a kid's cat's-meow outfit with a snip here, a silk rose there and a little tulle ruffle or three along the hem. This chapter offers some Pygmalion remakes just for your little lady. Learn to transform a dated petticoat and lace top into a budget-right flower girl's dress using your magic upcycling wand.

Je T'aime, Paris

Mommy's Chanel-like jacket has been retired from service but it is a hot new property for a preteen clothes-horse daughter. With a lavender bow in the back to nip it in and improve the fit, sassy little flowers on front, and the French phrase "I love you, Paris" beside the Eiffel Tower on the back, you have a drop-dead-darling spring jacket for a tween. Add a T-shirt and some jeans and the girl is ready to stroll down the Champs Élysées in style.

Materials

- Tweedy Chanel-style jacket
- 1½ yd. (1.4 m) lavender silk ribbon, 2 ¼ in. (5.7 cm) wide
- Assorted silk flowers
- Scrap paper and regular and colored pencils
- Muslin scraps for backing the writing and the tower
- Heart-shaped button
- Small amount of yarn for the words
- Embroidery thread or fine pearl cotton
- Sparkle ribbon for the Eiffel Tower
- Fabric glue
- Scrap of tulle

JACKET ATTRIBUTES ✳ **The Chanel-style jacket used for this project was a size 2. It had three seams in the back and fold-up sleeves, both attributes that made it a good candidate for this project. Three back seams lend themselves well to having sashes or belt ties attached so that the jacket can be drawn in to fit a child. Roll-up sleeves are an asset since they can be rolled a little higher for the young lady.**

Text

Decide where on the back of the garment you want to write your message. Write out the phrase "Je t'aime, Paris" in cursive on a piece of paper, then place it on the garment where you want it. Adjust the size of your script until you have the look you want.

Next, copy the script onto a scrap of muslin using a colored pencil. Take it to the sewing machine and sew over the cursive writing with straight stitches two or three times in the color of thread you want to use on the garment.

Now take the yarn you want to use for the script. Place the end of the yarn on the first letter of the first word and, using a straight stitch, begin sewing the yarn down over what you have already stitched. Once your entire script is written in yarn and stitched in straight stitch, stitch it again, this time using a narrow zigzag stitch to secure the yarn tightly to the script.

Now take the scrap of muslin with the script on it and pin it to your jacket just where you want it. Use embroidery thread or fine pearl cotton to attach the script to the jacket with hand-stitching. You can use an embroidery hoop if you wish to make this process easier. If your jacket is lined, be careful to not sew through the lining as you sew the script to the jacket. If necessary, release the lining at the bottom of the jacket so that you can get a hand inside the jacket. Just sew the lining hem back in place once you are finished.

Once the script is stitched to the jacket, trim around each letter with sharp embroidery scissors to eliminate the spare muslin, leaving only the cursive message. Use a heart—an iron-on heart, a button, or hand-embroidery—for the dot on the "i" in the word "Paris."

Eiffel Tower

First, find a sketch of the Eiffel Tower to use as a model to sketch your own on a piece of scrap paper. Hold the sketch to the back of the jacket and adjust the size, if needed, for a pleasing design. Place two layers of tulle over the pencil sketch. Take your sparkly ribbon and lay it carefully on top of the tulle, over the lines of your sketch, then pin it in place on the tulle. Lay the tulle on the jacket and pin it in place. Hand-stitch the Eiffel Tower to the jacket, taking the pins out as you go. Trim away the excess tulle around the design. Sew a button to the very top of the tower.

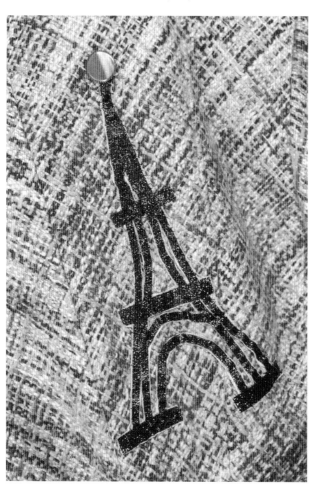

Buttons

Embellish the buttons on the front of the jacket with a variety of silk flowers. Hydrangeas and geraniums work great for this. Take the silk flowers apart and make your own hybrid flowers (see the directions for Frankenstein Flowers on page 7). Glue the flower petals together using tiny dots of fabric glue. Cut one small slit in the new hybrid flower to serve as a small button hole. Slip each flower over a button and tack it in place with needle and thread.

Sash

Pin one end of each of the two lengths of ribbon to the outer seams on the back of the jacket. Try it on Miss Paris and make sure that when you tie the sash, the jacket fits just right. Fold under and press a hem on the ends you are going to sew to the jacket so that they don't unravel later. Sew the sashes to the back of the jacket and tie in a bow.

Styling

• Skinny jeans or a pleated plaid wool skirt with leggings, paired with a white blouse with a Peter Pan collar, and Miss Paris is ready for school days—or weekend fun!

Tips

• Tween girls love to look a little sassy. This sweet pink and lavender jacket is sassy but still age appropriate.
• Sizes 0 and 2 are good candidates to upcycle for tween girls.

52 Pickup

Remember those boxy pastel linen shift dresses from the '80s? Bet if you rummage around in a closet or thrift shop you can turn up a pretty sherbet-hued linen dress lined in 100% polyester like this one. The lovely color, the fact that there was no extraneous trim, and the simple shape made this a perfect candidate to recycle from mom's closet to a little girl's closet. The generous length of linen is a great place to experiment with fashioning a "pickup" skirt at little or no cost. On top of that, the dress is way cute on the munchkin, and munchkin will love it.

Materials

- Lined linen sleeveless dress (must be lined)
- 3 rolls of colored tulle
- 2 colors of silky ribbon
- Knit sleeveless T-shirt or camisole
- Safety pins

Preparations

Rip out the stitches between the lining and the hem of the dress. Leave the lining sewn to the dress around the neck and arm openings.

Bodice

Put the dress on munchkin, then mark and pin where it should be taken in under the arms. Plan to pair the dress with a sleeveless T-shirt or camisole, but pin the side seam close enough to the body for modesty.

Turn both the dress and the lining wrong side out. You'll take the dress in under the arms by sewing the side seams in an A-line manner—a straight diagonal line down the side of the dress. If the dress has pockets which you want to preserve, take the side seams in only from the top of the pocket up to the underarm. Trim off the wedge of extra fabric where you took the dress in, then press the seams open. Turn the dress back right side out.

Put the dress back on munchkin and pin a deep inverted box pleat in the center of the neckline in the front and in the back. Make sure the two pleats are generous enough that the dress will be comfy for the girl. Securely sew the box pleats in place by stitching them down about 2 in. (5 cm) from the neckline. You will cover this stitching with embellishments later.

Skirt

Measure to see where you want the hem of the new dress to fall on your little girl, then cut the lining of the dress one inch longer than you want the actual finished dress to be (don't cut the top layer of the dress yet). Fold under the bottom edge of the lining ¼ in. (6 mm) and press. Pin this folded edge to bottom edge of the top layer of the dress. The lining will be several inches shorter than the linen. Machine stitch the two together along the hemline.

Now it's time for the pickups. The essence of the activity is to make a pinch of the linen and make sure you grab the lining in the pinch as well. Safety pin each pickup to the lining. This dress has seven pickups on the one side and eight on the other. Scatter the pickups so you have two or three across in three or four rows. Avoid making a pickup

where a pocket is. Again, try the dress on the child and make any necessary adjustments on the pickups. Tack the pickups in place with a tight zigzag stitch and remove the pins.

Embellishment

Using two colors of silky ribbon (I picked aqua to match the dress and hot pink to match the camisole underneath), make a big bow for one side of the dress. Use a safety pin to attach the bow to the dress, on top of the stitching on the neckline box pleat, so that you can remove the bow before washing the dress.

Using aqua, hot pink, and lime green tulle, make a nice flat tulle rose for the other side to cover the stitching on the box pleat. Use a little scrap of the linen you trimmed from the side seams to make leaves to tuck under the rose. Tack the rose and the leaves down to the dress.

Styling

• This dress makes a real statement on its own. It won't take much to polish it off. Some sandals and a smile will show off this creation nicely.

Tips

• If you are having trouble grabbing both the linen and the slippery lining when making the pickups, try using a plastic crochet hook to help poke up a hunk of both fabrics where you can grab them and safety pin them in place.

• See Chapter 1 for instructions for the tulle rose.

Lacy Lucy

Mom's special-occasion lace tunic served her well, but she was ready for a new look. What a boon this was for daughter dear! The dress portion of this project is super easy—no sewing is required. The pantaloons are not as simple, but they are still pretty easy. Store-bought lacy leggings could easily be substituted for the pantaloons to simplify this project. The giant shaggy flower could also be replaced with a no-sew remade silk flower. There is a whole world of possibilities out there for Little Lacy Lucy. She could go to a party or a special event or even sprinkle flower petals and granola down the aisle at an eco-friendly wedding.

Materials

- Woman's Battenburg lace tunic top
- Scraps of lining fabric for flower
- Vintage tatting and crochet for pantaloon trim
- Ivory tulle
- 3 yd. (2.7 m) silky ivory ribbon, 1 in. (2.5 cm) wide
- Upcycled muslin or other cotton fabric for pantaloons
- ½ yd. (0.5 m) elastic for waist and knees of pantaloons, ⅜ in. (1 cm) wide
- Pattern for pantaloons or crop pants
- Pin back

Dress

For this project, choose a tunic top with a lacy scoop neck that a ribbon can be threaded through. Thread the ribbon through the lace around the neck of the tunic, starting at the back center. Run it in and out of the neckline lace all the way around. Use the ribbon to gather the neckline to fit the child, then tie the two ends together in a bow once the dress is on the child. You may add a sleeveless T-shirt for the child to wear under the lace tunic for warmth, comfort, or modesty.

Pantaloons

For the pantaloons, use a remnant of muslin quilt backing or something comparable, like an old cotton sheet. The quilt backing worked great because it gave the pantaloons a little structure and loft. Just about any pattern for cropped pants with an elastic waistband will work for the pantaloons if you finish them with a ruffle around the legs. Using vintage crochet work with a little tulle underneath provides the finish flair on the pantaloons' legs.

Sew the pantaloons together following the pattern. Sew a casing at the waist and insert elastic to fit. Sew a 1 in. (2.5 cm) casing in the bottom of each leg. Choose the crochet or tatted lace for the leg edge. I used a 4 in. (10 cm) wide piece with swans on it, but there was not enough of it for both legs. For the second leg, a scalloped-edge lace that varied from 4 to 5 in. (10 to 13 cm) wide made a cute, funky companion. The lace pattern was completely different from the one on the other leg, but that was part of the charm. Sew the lace along the very bottom edge of the legs, gathering it a bit as you do so if the piece of lace is a little longer than the leg is wide. Using a safety pin, thread the ⅜ in. (1 cm) elastic through the leg casing and sew it together at a length that reins in the pantaloon leg snugly, but not tight enough to bug the wearer. Add a tulle ruffle under the lace to make the lace stand out a little. Sew ivory ribbon around each leg along the top of the lace trim, then ice the cake by tying two nice matching silky bows, one on each front knee.

Flower

This is a scrap dragon flower made from silky lining scraps. See page 7 for directions.

Styling

• Ivory tights and black patent leather Mary Jane slippers or soft buttery leather lace-up boots would be perfect with this ensemble.

• If you are in a cold climate, an ivory turtleneck or crew-neck long-sleeved T-shirt would help avoid a chill.

Tips

• Search for the perfect tunic to upcycle—it needs a lacy neckline through which you can thread the ribbon, allowing you to alter the size of the dress without making a stitch.

• Lacy ivory tights or leggings would also work with this ensemble if you don't want to sew the pantaloons.

Degas's Little Dancer

Have you ever seen Edgar Degas's sculpture *La Petite Danseuse de Quatorze Ans (The Little Fourteen-Year-Old Dancer)*? This lovely recycled creation instantly brings that sculpture to mind. Two of mommy's castaway items are upcycled in this lovely special-occasion confection: The bodice is a no-longer-worn sleeveless top made of stretchy lace, while the skirt is a blast-from-the-past pale pink tiered lace and cotton vintage petticoat joined to a beige cotton sleeveless tank top. The ethereal ivory and pale pink colors looked like they were meant to be together. The stretchy lace top fit a young girl without modification and the drop-waisted tiered skirt could be cropped to the desired length. Those qualities made the set perfect for upcycling for a little dancer, a flower girl, or any child yearning to be a fairy.

COLORS * The ivory/ballet pink color scheme for the Little Dancer's dress is hard to resist, but this could be made in many different color palettes—think pale shades of blue and lavender or mint green and sky blue. The colors of the top and skirt you have to work with will help you choose the coloring of the embellishments. Working in a monochromatic palette with a lot of subtle variations in color gives the piece an Impressionistic look that you may love—or your upcycled items may guide you to work in a more colorful palette such as red and orange. As designer, it's your call.

Materials

- Woman's stretch lace sleeveless top
- Dropped-waist tiered skirt or petticoat
- Nude-colored sleeveless T-shirt or camisole
- Roll of ivory tulle
- Vintage package of 100% rayon ivory seam binding tape
- Vintage odds and ends of ribbon—organza and satin
- Odds and ends of old millinery or silk flowers
- Crochet hook
- Candle and matches
- Liquid fabric softener

Preparing the Overskirt Elements

Split the vintage ivory rayon seam binding tape into two long strips. Start by cutting the end of the tape in half with scissors, then take those two ends and tear the tape into two long strips. Use vintage tape, if you can get it, for this project; the vintage tape rips beautifully due to the age of the fabric. The frayed edge gives it a lovely ephemeral look.

Next, prepare some ribbons for the overskirt. This project used a sack of 1 yd. (0.9 m) pieces of ³/₄ in. (1.9 cm) wide strips of organza ribbon that came from a recycle center. Split each length of ribbon in half as for the seam tape. Rip away until you have about fifty of these nice, frayed gossamer streamers.

Tulle straight off the roll was way too new and pretty looking when paired with the recycled clothing being used for this project. It needed a little touch of shabby chic. To achieve this vintage look, cut your tulle strips into strips

2 to 3 ft. (60 to 90 cm) long. Don't measure the exact length of the strips—just estimate. Cut the ends diagonally so that the dress will have a more organic look. Once you have cut about two dozen tulle strips, use a lighted candle to singe them a little (see page 10). Singe all the exterior edges of the tulle strips, then singe a few quick holes down the center of each strip. The strips should look tatty along the edges and a little Swiss-cheesy down the middle.

The next step is to soften the tulle a little so that it is not so stiff and clingy. Dilute some liquid fabric softener in warm water and soak the holey tulle strips in the fabric softener overnight. Without rinsing the tulle strips, lay them on a towel to dry.

Make flowers to tie onto the overskirt streamers by taking apart store-bought silk flowers and harvesting the most delicate and pleasing parts.

Assembling the Overskirt

Once you have all your overskirt elements ready, divide them into four groups. Attach each shabby tulle streamer to the bottom edge of the lace bodice as follows: Fold the streamer in half. Use a crochet hook to push the fold in

the streamer through a lacy hole in the lower edge of the bodice. Using your left hand, hold open the loop you have pushed through the lace. With your right hand, poke the two tails of the streamer through the loop and pull them tight. This will "tie" them to the bottom of the bodice.

Continue to attach the streamers around the bottom edge of the bodice in this way, putting about six strips in each quarter of the edge, so that the tulle streamers form a sort of tutu. Attach strips of the torn rayon bias tape and torn organza ribbon in the spaces between the tulle strips. Run an occasional streamer end through the center of a modified flower part and tie it in a knot.

Rip short strips of narrow tulle to make little snippets of tulle to tie to the ends of ribbons and tattered tulle here and there.

Flowers for the Neckline

Take a 6 in. (15 cm) square of tulle, fold it in half, cut it, then fold it again to make two 3 in. (8 cm) tulle squares to serve as base for your flowers. Repeat for as many bases as you need. Topstitch pink or ivory ribbon to the bases in circles to form small flat rosettes. You will need enough pink and ivory roses to alternate all around the neckline of your ballerina's dress. The project shown here required twelve tulle rosettes. Tear some green tulle to add leaves to some of the roses.

Underdress

Cut off the bottom three tiers from a can-can petticoat or tiered skirt to use as the underskirt. Pin, then stitch these three tiers to the bottom of a beige cotton camisole. Adjust the underskirt/camisole combination as needed to fit perfectly under the embellished lace overdress.

Tips

• Make extra tulle roses and put them on a headband for your little ballerina.
• Take your time on this project—there are many steps to it, but they're fun.

Styling

• Ivory tights and some pink ballet slippers are just what the stylist ordered for this little dancer. For events requiring "real shoes," ivory ballet flats substitute well.
• If this ensemble is for a photoshoot, adding a tiny lacey nosegay, like dancers get at the end of a recital, would be perfection.
• Degas's Little Dancer has a lovely silk ribbon holding back her ponytail. Why not copy the master?

CHAPTER 6

Scrap Bag Mash-Up

Using scraps to mend textiles is an age-old tradition. Using the scraps to create new clothing is a less ancient tradition. With just a sack of surplus linings, you really can create some charming outfits. Grab your scrap bags and make a couple of feisty skirts, a dress for a wood sprite, and even a charmer of a dress from Scarlett's old curtains. You'd never guess what beautiful raiment can be made from a bag or two of old fabric scraps!

Scarlett's Curtains

Didn't you love the part in *Gone With the Wind* where Scarlett makes a beautiful dress out of the living room curtains? Well, why not relive that amazing moment in fashion history using the scrap bag? What could be more fun? This dress was cut and sewn from a lonely faded curtain panel of French toile from the Reagan era. Don't worry about making sure everything matches on this project. The toile print makes a bold statement that the other linens in white and pastel colors complement nicely. The colorful appliquéd rose on the hand-towel apron and the little pops of color on the white pockets tie this dress together nicely. The linen napkin side panels in muted pastel colors serve as nice grace notes. This is a pastiche of scraps that otherwise would have been considered beyond use.

Materials

- Vintage curtains (one long panel or two café curtain panels)
- Vintage hand towel
- Scraps of vintage pillow cases for pockets
- Scraps of tatting and vintage hankies for hemline
- Scraps of fabric with doll graphics
- Scrap of lightweight cotton for bodice lining
- Rickrack for bodice neck trim
- 3 buttons
- 3 in. (8 cm) sew-on Velcro strip
- Bodice pattern
- Two 16 in. (41 cm) square linen napkins
- Ribbon for bow
- Silk flowers and silk flower petals

Preparations

Hand-wash all the vintage linens and let them air-dry. Press them.

Skirt

Because the curtain was an old style, it was only 36 in. (91 cm) wide; I had enough of it for two panels, but the skirt of the dress needed to be fuller than that. I used two worn-out linen napkins as side panels to expand the fullness of the skirt. Cut your curtain into two lengths equal to the length of the two napkins plus an extra 1½ in. (3.8 cm) to form a hem on the bottom front and back edges. The napkins won't need to be hemmed since they have a finished edge. Turn under ¼ in. (6 mm) and press along the raw edges of both curtain panels. Turn under again and press until the curtain panels are the same length as the napkins. Machine stitch this hem.

Making sure the fabric pattern is right side up, sew the front and back curtain panels to the linen napkins. Press the four side seams.

Bodice

Using a bodice pattern that fits your little Scarlett, cut out the bodice from the remaining part of the curtains. Cut a bodice lining from cotton or linen scraps. Sew the bodice together following the directions on the pattern. Sew rickrack around the bodice neckline. Turn and press the bodice. Sew three little strips of Velcro at the back to serve as closures, then sew three pretty buttons on the outside of the closure just for decoration.

Embellishment

Hemline

Cut your piece of crochet or tatting into 2 equal sections, one for the front center panel and one for the back center panel. It is okay if the pieces of crochet are not quite as wide as the curtain panels. You are going to fill them in with the corners of hankies. Secure the side edges of the crochet by serging them or by using a dense zigzag stitch to keep them from unraveling.

Cut the corners from old white hankies (save the centers to use later). Press the raw edge of each hankie wedge under twice, then pin it to an area on the hem where you do not have trim. Sew the hankies in place.

Sew ready-made ribbon flowers and silk flower petals at each intersection between hankies around the hem of the skirt.

Apron

Choose a hand towel that accents your curtain panels to use as an apron for the dress. Make pockets for the apron from scraps of old pillow cases that have crochet or tatting trim. Cut two pieces twice the size you want for the pockets (mine were 3 by 8 in. [8 by 20 cm]). Fold them in half with wrong sides together and sew around the edge, leaving an opening. Turn each pocket right side out, then stitch closed the opening that you used to turn the pocket. Leave the crochet edge on the top of the pocket. Prepare the patches of doll fabric by turning the four edges under and pressing. Pin the patches onto the pockets, then sew around the edge to attach them. Sew the pockets onto the apron.

Joining Bodice to Skirt

Machine baste the apron to the center front panel across the top of the waist. Using the sewing maching, sew a line of basting stitches all the way around the top of the skirt. Pull on the threads to gather the skirt until it fits the bodice. Pin and then sew the bodice to the skirt. Turn the dress wrong side out, pin the bodice lining in place, and sew by hand.

Styling

• Add some white leggings or tights and some black patent leather Mary Jane shoes and Scarlett is ready for the garden party.
• In winter, add a long-sleeved, Peter Pan-collared blouse to keep Scarlett warm.

Tips

• Keep a bag of hankie scraps for moments like this. Never throw away a scrap of hankie—they are as scarce as hen's teeth.

Sunday Vest and Ombre Skirt

Remember saving something special to wear as your Sunday best? Upcycling a little something for your sweet girl can be a very satisfying and thrifty project. The skirt looks complicated but it isn't as bad as it looks. The vest is a super easy project that you don't even need a sewing machine to make. What young miss does not want an ombre shaded skirt to sashay about in? The premise is simple. All you need is a sack of unwanted, unused silky lining fabric.

Materials

Skirt
• Scrap bag of silky lining scraps in 7 shades
  of the same color
• Piece of chalk
• A-line skirt pattern (optional)
• Elastic for waistband
• Rotary cutter and mat

Vest
• 100% wool sweater vest
• 2 bias strips of lining fabric (left over from
  the skirt project)

Skirt

Use the lining fabric you have the most of to cut the base skirt from. The one I used had a designer name printed all over the fabric, so I made the base skirt using the "wrong" side of the lining, obscuring the name. Cut two matching pieces, one each for the front and back of the skirt; each should be one skirt length plus one inch for the bottom hem and three additional inches for the waistband casing. This skirt was cut 22 in. (56 cm) long.

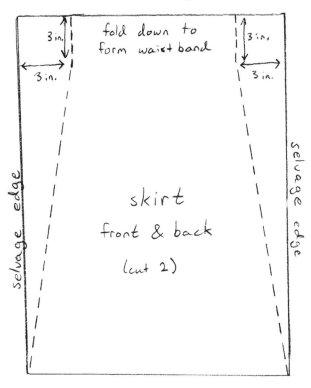

Trace and cut out the pieces of an A-line skirt pattern from the base fabric, or create your own simple A-line skirt as follows: Lay out the fabric, folded in half lengthwise. Measure in 3 in. (8 cm) from each side at one end, mark with chalk, and extend this line 3 in. (8 cm) in from the edge of the fabric; this will form the waistband casing. Now use the chalk to draw the sides of the skirt, going in a straight diagonal line from the bottom edge of the waisband to the bottom corners of the fabric. Cut along the lines you just drew.

Sew up the two side seams of the skirt and press the seams open. Fold the bottom hem under ¼ in. (6 mm) and press. Fold under again, press, and pin. Sew the bottom hem and press once more.

Fold under the top of the skirt ¼ in. (6 mm) and press. Fold over the top again, 1½ in. (3.8 cm) this time, and press and pin; this forms the casing for the elastic waistband. Sew along the bottom edge of the casing, leaving a 1½ in. (3.8 cm) opening through which to insert the elastic. Press but do not insert the elastic yet.

Making the Strips

Fold your lining pieces so that you can cut bias strips approximately 2 in. (5 cm) wide from them. Cut strips from a variety of different shades of the same color. This skirt used seven different colors.

Sewing the Strips

Now you are ready to sew the ombre strips to the skirt. Sort your strips by color into piles. Begin at the very bottom of the skirt by sewing one of the darkest bias strips to the base skirt, starting about 1 in. (2.5 cm) above the hemline, just behind of the left side seam. If you want a hint of a ruffled look to your skirt, as in the one shown here, take a tiny tuck every few inches as you sew the strip down. When you near the end of the first strip, overlay it slightly with another strip of the same color and keep sewing. Continue sewing down ruffles in an upward spiral around the skirt. Sew about three strips of the darkest color down before moving on to the next shade. Continue in this manner from darkest to lightest. The last row of strips should end up directly under the stitch line of the casing for the elastic waist. Complete the skirt by inserting the elastic in the waistband and fitting it to your child. Stitch the ends of the elastic together, then sew the casing shut.

Styling

- Dark brown tights and an ivory turtleneck would make this a great winter outfit, paired with boots.
- This skirt, without the vest, when paired with a natural colored T-shirt or lace top, makes a lovely special event ensemble.

Tips

- Use patterned lining with the wrong side out so that you just see the color, not the pattern. Two of the fabrics on this skirt had designer names printed in vivid colors on the right side. Can you spot them?
- Make sure the end of each strip is cut on the diagonal. Allow the ends to fray a little to add texture to the design.
- Embellish the waistband of the skirt with a round flower or two, some shaggy roses, or fabric roses with ribbon and lace.

Vest

Felt the sweater vest to a size that fits your child. This one zipped down the front, so I removed the zipper once the vest was felted to size. Cut two bias strips of lining fabric about 3 in. (8 cm) wide to use to close the vest. Fold and press under one end of each strip, then fold and press under once more. Pin, then sew the two bias strips to the center front opening of the vest. Use these two streamers to tie a bow to close the vest.

Ivory Wood Sprite

This wood sprite's dress was created from nothing but scraps and leftovers. The starting place was a tub of scraps of white and ivory fabric and bits of ribbons. The ivory skirt shape and bodice were cut from larger scraps, but many of the embellishments on the dress were used in exactly the shapes they were found in. The scraps led the design process. Left-over bits of lining fabric lent themselves to the roses on the tiara, along with the scraps of tulle and the pearls from a broken necklace. Could this dress be any more perfect for a little wood sprite? With a few scraps of fabric and a little creativity, she's ready for her sylvan glen close-up.

Materials

- Tulle, recycled ribbons, pearls, and buttons
- Scraps of ivory silk, cotton, linen, scrim, and other fabrics
- Empire bodice pattern
- Long picot-edged ribbon for sash
- Velcro tape
- Pearl beads from old necklaces and other jewelry

Bodice

Cut out the pieces for the bodice lining from a muslin scrap, then cut the pieces for the bodice itself from raw silk, making it larger all around than the lining. Sew up the shoulder and underarm seams on both the bodice and the lining. Sew the lining to the bodice around the neckline, then turn and press that seam. Run basting stitches up the back center seams and side seams of the bodice to use to gather it along these seams so that it fits the lining. Spritz water on the raw silk and crush it into shape so that it fits the lining. Let dry, then blind stitch the creases to the lining by hand so that the silk stays crushed in place. Sew the side seams of the lining, then the side seams of the bodice. Sew the center back seam of the lining, stopping 3 in. (8 cm) from the top; do the same with the bodice. Turn under the seam allowance along the unfinished edges, then top-stitch the lining and bodice together along this edge. Sew Velcro tape to both sides to close the opening, then add a pearl button at the top for show.

Skirt

Cut out pieces of fabric for an A-line skirt, making sure the top of the skirt is larger around than the bottom of the bodice so that the skirt will be fuller than the bodice. Sew the side seams. Rip 2 in. (5 cm) wide strips of assorted ivory fabrics and run a basting line down a long side of each. Pull the basting threads to gather the ruffles.

Put a shirt-tail hem in the skirt by pressing ¼ in. (6 mm) of fabric under twice and then stitching in place. Next, begin adding the ruffles to the bottom of the skirt. Stitch down the first ruffle starting about 1 in. (2.5 cm) from the bottom of the skirt. Don't pin, just start sewing, going slightly "uphill" in a spiral as you continue around the dress. When one ruffle ends, add another, overlapping it a little with the old one. Continue to spiral around the skirt until you have about three or four rows of ruffles in a variety of fabrics.

Cut a second A-line skirt from scrim or another transparent, textural fabric, making it a few inches longer than the first skirt. Sew the side seams. Beginning at the bottom of this skirt, take horizontal darts in a random fashion around the skirt. Keep adding darts until the overskirt reaches only from the empire waistline to the ruffles on the first skirt. Sew the scrim skirt to the base skirt around the top edge, then sew a line of basting stitches around the top of this double skirt and pull the threads to gather the skirt so that it fits the bodice. Pin this double skirt to the bodice, then sew.

Embellishment

Tear up 2 in. (5 cm) wide strips of ivory scraps for embellishment ruffles. Run basting stitches down the length of one edge of rectangle strips and pull threads to ruffle them. Run basting stitches down the centers of wedge-shaped pieces to make acanthus leaves. Sew these embellishments above the highest row of hem ruffles to camouflage the raw edge.

Embellish the scrim skirt with assorted scraps. Take odd pieces of the fabrics and tie them in simple knots, then tack them to the dress. Make roses from tulle, knit, and woven cloth scraps (see page 6 for instructions); sew them to the ruffles.

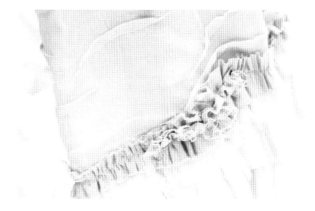

Sash

Embellish a wide picot-edged ribbon to make a sash for the dress. Make roses from a variety of silky fabrics (see page 6 for directions) and sew them to the ribbon. Sew pearls from old broken necklaces to the sash between the roses in a random pattern. Sew loops of fabric or ribbon to the bodice of the dress at the side and back seams to hold the sash in place.

Tiara

Twist the lightweight wire into a circle several strands thick. Wrap the wire circle in tulle, then embellish it with bits and bobs of singed tulle, ribbons, pearls, and buttons.

Styling

• Ivory slippers or ballet shoes are all a sprite needs to be party ready in this dress.
• A basket of flower petals, and the sprite is ready to be the flower girl at any wedding.

Tips

• Leave symmetry behind!
• Use rolls of tulle from the bridal supply section.
• Rip, don't cut, the fabric for ruffles for more natural-looking frayed edges.
• The dress is perfect for a photo op, a first communion, or a special holiday event.

Silver Linings

Every cloud has its silver lining—and hopefully your scrap bag does, too! The scrap bag is an amazing source of potential projects. Just a little bit of this and little bit of that swirled together with bits and bobs of lace and trim can produce a show-stopping piece of fiber art. Pair this over-the-top skirt with a simple wooly corset and a plain gray T-shirt and you might need sunglasses to gaze upon this sterling-silver ensemble.

Materials

- Gray silky lining in 6 different shades, including one piece large enough to make a skirt from
- Assorted scraps of gray fabric
- Bits of rayon bias tape, linen strips, upholstery trims, lace, and other embellishments
- Elastic for waistband
- Silver tulle, 6 in. (15 cm) wide
- A-line skirt pattern or make your own
- Gray T-shirt
- Bottom section of a felted 100% wool dark gray pullover sweater
- Chalk

Preparations

Start by cutting the lining scraps into bias strips 2 to 3 in. (5 to 8 cm) wide. You will have all different lengths of strips—short, medium and long—and that is just fine. Cut both ends of each strip on the diagonal. Most of the strips will serve as ruffles to embellish the lower two-thirds of the skirt and a few will trim the upper third. Make sure you have several shades of gray and several different textures. Cut or rip one strip 5 in. (13 cm) wide from the darkest of your grays.

Skirt

Cut out an A-line skirt that will fit your child from a piece of gray lining fabric. You can use a pattern or you can make your own. Sew the side seams and hem the skirt. Fold under ¼ in. (6 mm) along the top edge of the skirt and press, then fold under and press 1½ in. (3.8 cm) to form a waistband casing. Pin, then sew along the bottom edge of the casing, leaving a 1½ in. (3.8 cm) opening for inserting the elastic. Do not add the elastic yet, so that you will have a completely flat surface to embellish.

Guide Ruffles

Lay the skirt out, with the back side up, and chalk a curved line from the right-hand side seam (about 6 to 8 in. [15 to 20 cm] above the hem) up across the back of the skirt and back down to hit the other side seam about 6 to 8 in. (15 to 20 cm) above the hem, forming a blunt mountain shape. Draw a steeper arc up from the left side of this mountain and across the side seam to the front of the skirt, then slope it unevenly down the front of the skirt to the bottom left corner. These guide lines establish the pattern of embellishment for the skirt.

Take your large, dark lining strip and sew it along the second chalk line. Let the diagonal end of the strip hang down below the edge of the skirt as you begin stitching it down. Take a ¼ in. (6 mm) pin tuck every few inches as you sew the strip down, so that the strip makes a ruffle.

Once the first strip is sewn down, pull more strips in a variety of shades and sizes and begin to fill in the section of the skirt between your guide strip and the hem. Fold back the guide ruffle so that you can start right below it and add rows of ruffles until you have filled in the space between the guide ruffle and the hem of the skirt in this one section. Include a ruffle of new tulle within this section. You can singe this tulle ruffle to make it wispier.

Now turn the skirt over to the back and sew a second wide lining strip on the first chalk line, tucking it as you go as with the first one. Fill in the area below with the narrower strips. Vary the colors and the textures of the strips and tuck them as you go to produce ruffles. Continue adding ruffles, filling in the entire area under the guide lines as if you were planting rows of corn.

Acanthus Leaves

Cut several wedges of fabric from your stash of scraps. Your widest wedge should be about 3 in. (8 cm) wide at the wide end and about 8 to 12 in. (20 to 30 cm) long. Run basting stitches down the center of each wedge and pull to make the wedges into ruching. Set aside these ruched wedges while you prepare the top third of the skirt. (See page 10 for more on preparing these elements.)

Top of Skirt

Recycled sleeve lining from tailored jackets makes a perfect base for embellishment for the top of the skirt. Lay a piece of sleeve lining with raw, ripped edges on a section of the top third of the skirt and pin it in place. It should be taller and wider than the section of skirt to which you are pinning it so that it ends up being fuller than the actual skirt. Lay another sleeve lining down on the back of the skirt top and pin it in place. Topstitch these two sleeve remnants in place just under the waistband casing and up against the ruffled area of the skirt.

Now embellish the top area of the skirt with bits and bobs of rayon bias tape, linen strips, upholstery trims, lace, and the remaining bias strips of lining you cut earlier. Use the chalk to draw in some very lazy S-curves, about 4 in. (10 cm) apart, snaking around the top third of the skirt. Choose one of the trims and stitch it down to a chalked S (sew down the center of a narrow strip or down both edges of a wider strip). Continue to add strips, capturing the looseness of the sleeve lining you have topstitched onto this section of the skirt so that there is a subtle depth to this appliqué treatment. Be sure to include raw edges when you can.

More Embellishment

Take this skirt over the top by adding more embellishment. Add tulle tufts wherever you want to add a little loft to the skirt ruffles. You can add a little bouquet of strips of lace, tulle, and lining scraps to either the back and or front of the skirt, or a lovely fabric rose made of silky lining. See Chapter 1 (pages 6–10) for directions for creating these and other embellishments.

Corset

The corset is easy to make. Start with the lower part of an already-felted pullover sweater that will fit around your child with room left over. Slice it open down one side seam and fit it on your child with the opening in the front. Fold under the two cut edges and pin in place so that the corset fits your child with a few inches of space between the two front edges. Sew the two folded-under edges in place using the machine. Rip two strips of lining fabric about 1½ in. (3.8 cm) wide and fold them into thirds to make strips ½ in. (1.3 cm) wide, then press. Pin each folded strip to the inside of each edge of corset opening and tack it down to make four loops on each side to use to lace the corset. Rip a strip of lining fabric 2 to 3 in. (5 to 8 cm) wide to use as the corset lace. Lace the corset like a shoe, starting at the top or the bottom (your choice) and ending with a big bow.

T-Shirt Top

A simple gray knit top from the thrift store or big box store is perfect to put with this wild and crazy skirt and killer corset. It tones it down nicely.

Styling

• Tights, black boots, and a faux leather jacket might suit your little sweetie.

Tips

• Use the lining fabric on both sides so that one fabric gives two different looks. One side will be shinier than the other; some fabrics may have a logo printed on one side for an even more different look.

CHAPTER 7

Upcycling Vintage Linens

Have you ever seen a little girl dressed in grandmother's guest towels? You're about to! This chapter is full of examples and directions for charming and zany clothes made from vintage linens. The kitchen towels, linen napkins, and tablecloths used in these clothes incorporate memories from times gone by and a very different way of life. Take the old and obsolete and make it new and useful for today through upcycling.

Tuesday at Windsor

Who doesn't have a linen tea towel that was a travel souvenir from a famous place? These towels tend to hang out in the linen drawer forever with the sticker tag indicating that they are 100% pure linen still stuck on them. They are so colorful (or colourful, depending on their country of origin), charming, and far too beautiful for the landfill. Pair a souvenir tea towel with a "days of the week" dish towel, some scrap bag filler, two cocktail napkins, and some wacky trim and you have a too-cute-for-words skirt that will turn heads for all the right reasons.

Materials

- Linen souvenir dish towel
- Day-of-the-week dish towel
- 2 red linen cocktail napkins
- Linen or cotton scraps for side panel fillers
- Hankie for apron
- Trim for embellishment
- Ribbon and safety pin for bow
- $7/8$ in. (2.2 cm) bias tape for casing for elastic waistband
- Elastic

Preparations

First, select the centerpiece towels for your creation. The souvenir towel used here has a landscape or horizontal orientation, while the second dish towel has a portrait orientation. Depending on the orientation of your towels, you may need to add some filler panels to one or both towels to give you the needed width. The filler could be more tea towels or just a remnant from the scrap bag.

For this project, some yellow and white chevron fabric from the scrap bag made a charming partner to the centerpiece towel, but the scrap was not long enough. Two well-worn red linen cocktail napkins, cut in half, made perfect flounces to add length to the filler panels.

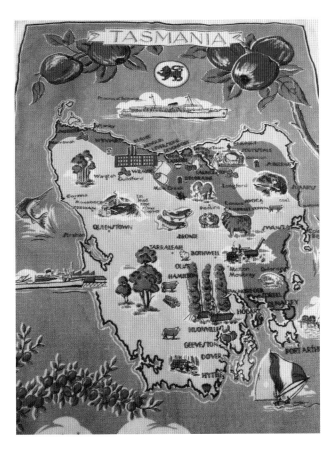

Skirt

Cut the two red napkins in half horizontally, then sew basting stitches across the raw edges. Pull the basting stitches to gather the napkins until they fit the bottom edges of the side panels. Stitch two gathered napkin halves to the lower edge of each side panel. Press the seam and then stitch some trim over the seam where the napkins meet the panels. Pin the finished panels to the front and back center panels and sew the side seams. Press seams open.

Choose a handkerchief to make a decorative apron for the day-of-the-week side of the skirt. Cut the hankie in half horizontally and baste it to the top edge of the skirt.

Next, make a casing for the elastic waistband. Stitch the bias tape to the top edge of the skirt with a ¼ in. (6 mm) seam allowance. Turn the bias tape to the wrong side and pin it in place, then sew, leaving an opening to insert the elastic. Pin a safety pin to one end of the elastic and use it to thread it through the casing. Fit the skirt comfortably to your child, then sew the elastic together and close the opening in the casing.

Embellishment

Both the front and the back of this little skirt were cute so they each needed a ribbon bow so either one could be the front. Tie two lengths of red grosgrain into bows. Pin the bows to the waistband with safety pins so you can remove them before washing the skirt.

Styling

• This bit of whimsy is darling with a red T-shirt with white stripes and a pair of red tights or leggings. Pretty ballet flats or Mary Janes will work beautifully.

Tips

• Pick up any remnant if it is in your general color palette and you love, love, love the design. For less than a buck you can have a back-up scrap on hand that you know is one that works for your design aesthetic.

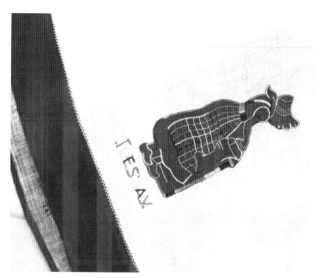

Blue Onion Frock

Everyone loves blue and white dishes, so vintage linens honoring blue and white china are plentiful. This creation started with a lovely Blue Onion–pattered linen dish towel. It still had its Pure Linen sticker on it—it had never been used. After thirty or more years on the shelf, the tea towel needed a place in the sun. Three sweet vintage blue and white cotton placemats turned on their ends and sewn together made the second half of the skirt. Some rickrack, some ribbons, and some silk flowers, and it was a blue and white charmer.

Materials

- Linen dish towel (landscape orientation)
- 3 cotton placemats (portrait orientation)
- End of a small dresser scarf for apron
- End of a larger dresser scarf for bodice front
- $\frac{7}{8}$ in. (2.2 cm) wide bias tape
- Ribbon for straps and bows
- Napkin for bodice back
- Bodice pattern
- Scrap fabric for bodice lining
- Flowers
- Wide rickrack

Preparations

Wash, air-dry, and press the linens you will be using.

Bodice

Cut out a bodice front from one embroidered end of a dresser scarf, carefully centering the embroidered pattern on the bodice (save the other end of the scarf to use in another project). Cut a bodice back from a matching napkin, and a front and back lining from any scrap fabric. Sew together the side seams of the bodice and lining and press.

Cut four lengths of coordinating-color ribbon for straps—two for the front and two for the back. Leave each strap long enough to serve as half a strap plus plenty of length to tie a bow. Cut the outside end of each ribbon on the diagonal; cut each end that will be attached to the bodice straight across. Pin the four straight ends of the ribbons to the four corners of the top of the bodice so they will be sewn into the seam when you sew the bodice and the lining together.

With wrong sides out, pin the bodice to the lining along the top edge, then sew. Clip the seams, press, and turn right side out. Turn under and press $\frac{5}{8}$ in. (1.6 cm) along the lower edge of the assembled bodice and lining.

Skirt

Sew the three placemats together along their long sides to make one long rectangle. Pin the two short ends of the tea towel to the long string of three placemats. If the placemats are slightly shorter than the towel, sew a strip of bias tape to their top edge to give them the extra height they need. When everything is lined up, sew the side seams.

Place the vintage dresser scarf in the center of the front of the skirt for an apron. Sew it in place, then cut off the surplus scarf fabric.

Sew two rows of basting stitches around the top edge of the skirt. Pull the threads to gather the skirt until it fits the bodice. Finish the bottom edge of the skirt by sewing a strip of rickrack to the underside of bottom edge of the skirt.

Embellishment

Use silk flowers and buttons to trim the bodice front where the straps meet it. Sew rickrack to the inside of the top edge of the bodice for trim. Try the dress on your little one and tie the straps at just the right level, then hand-sew the bows so they stay. Add another bow and silk flower to the center front just for fun.

Styling

• White leggings with a lacy edge seem just right with this homage to blue and white china. How about some red kid Mary Janes for her little tootsies?

Tips

• Somebody in your family is hanging on to some lovely pure linen tea towels that they would love to share with you to make such a useful and environmentally green little frock. Ask around.

• What possible use is one single linen napkin? Use it for the bodice!

Blue Delft Tunic Top

What to do with four luncheon-sized blue and white napkins, too nice to use as dust cloths but of no earthly use in today's lifestyle? Make a peppy little top for muffin! Add in one end of a dresser scarf for a bodice, the end of another small dresser scarf for an apron, and some bits and bobs of ribbons, trim, and flowers and you have a cute little tunic top! Pair it with jeans, shorts, or leggings—or, better still, make a circle skirt out of an old round tablecloth for a special occasion–worthy vintage winner!

Materials

- 4 luncheon-size napkins
- Larger dresser scarf
- Smaller dresser scarf
- Napkin for bodice back
- Scraps of muslin or another cotton or linen napkin for the bodice lining
- Bodice pattern
- Ribbon for bodice straps
- Wide rickrack
- Flowers

Bodice

Cut out the bodice front from one end of the dresser scarf, carefully centering the embroidered pattern on the bodice. Cut out the back bodice from a matching cloth napkin and cut the lining from scrap fabric or another napkin. Sew the side seams on the bodice and lining and press.

Cut four lengths of coordinating-color ribbon for straps—two for the front and two for the back. Leave each strap long enough to serve as half a strap plus plenty of length to tie a bow. Cut the outside end of each ribbon on the diagonal; cut each end that will be attached to the bodice straight across. Pin the four straight ends of the ribbons to the four corners of the top of the bodice so they will be sewn into the seam when you sew the bodice and the lining together.

With wrong sides out, pin the bodice and the lining together and sew along the top edge. Clip the seams, press, and turn right side out. Turn under and press ⅝ in. (1.6 cm) along the lower edge of the assembled bodice and lining.

Tunic Top Skirt

Sew the four napkins together in a pleasing order by overlapping the edges about ⅜ in. (1 cm) and topstitching each seam. (No need to sew a regular seam and press open.) Sew rickrack around the inside of the bottom edge of the skirt so that it peeks out beyond the bottom of the skirt. Stitch basting stitches around the top of the skirt and pull the threads to gather the skirt to a size that will fit the lower edge of the bodice. With right sides together, sew the skirt to the bodice, then sew the lining to the bodice-skirt seam by hand.

Embellishment

Sew the rickrack to the inside of the top edge of the bodice so that half of it shows along the top edge. Trim the top with some silk flowers that complement the embroidery on the dresser scarf bodice.

Try the top on your little girl and tie the straps at just the right level, then hand-sew the bows so they stay.

Styling

- Jeans, a jeans skirt, or denim leggings make a great companion to this little top. In cold weather, add a white shirt or a chambray shirt under it.

Tips

- Oh, for Pete's sake! Surely you have four luncheon napkins from Granny that you are hoarding. Resist the temptation to hoard, and make something useful and charming for her great-granddaughter instead!

Magic Mushroom

In the '60s and '70s, avocado green and harvest gold were very popular colors. Those two colors reigned in kitchen appliances and other decorative items. This never-used magic mushroom linen tea towel in that color scheme was too fun a graphic to not make an appearance after 40-plus years in storage.

Materials

- Graphic linen towel
- 2 linen hand towels
- Remnant from the scrap bag for bodice
- Remnant from the scrap bag for bodice lining
- Remnant of green net (the old-fashioned stiff kind still sold by the yard)
- Remnant of green lace edging
- Remnant of polka-dot grosgrain ribbon
- Rickrack
- Assorted green buttons
- Bodice pattern

Preparations

Cut the vintage linen towel in half so that both halves can be used with their design upright, one half for the front of the skirt and the other for the back. Choose two linen hand towels for the side panels to make the skirt fuller.

Bodice

Cut out the bodice front and back from a napkin or scraps of fabric. Cut the lining from another napkin or from scrap muslin. Sew the side seams of the lining and bodice, then pin the pieces together with wrong sides out. Sew along the top edge, turn right side out, and press.

Skirt

Pin the two main towel panels to the side panels, lining up the lower edges. Sew the side seams, then trim the top edge of the skirt so all the panels are the same length. Stitch two lines of basting stitches around the top of the skirt and pull the threads to gather the skirt to fit the bodice.

Pin the skirt to the bodice, then sew.

Embellishment

The kelly green net remnant adds thirty-four cents worth of color to the hemline. Fold the net in half, then in half again, and again. Once you have one long snake of green net, run basting stitches down the long open edge. Pull the basting stitches to gather the strip of net to fit the bottom edge of the dress.

Gather a strip of pea-green lace, pin it to the bottom edge of the skirt, under the green net, and sew it in place. Sew assorted green buttons to the top front bodice. Cut two lengths of wide spotted grosgrain ribbon for the shoulder straps and sew them in place on the wrong side

of the bodice. Sew two rows of green rickrack over the skirt-bodice seam. Make a perky bow from the same ribbon and sew it to the center front where the skirt meets the bodice.

Styling

- Not a lot of additional styling is necessary with this wild and crazy magic mushroom frock. How about flip-flops and a giant pinky ring?
- For cooler weather, add leggings and a shirt underneath the jumper.

Tips

- Sometimes the print design on the vintage tea towel is so wacky or whimsical you just want to cut loose with really over-the-top embellishment. Go with it! From a kid's point of view, less is not more. More is more!
- Pick up remnants of net and tulle when you see them for fifty cents or less. They pack a big wallop for little money.

My Little Poodle

The '50s and '60s produced some beautiful graphic linen tea towels. Some of these towels were so pretty to their owners that they were never used. I found this beautiful poodle languishing at an estate sale with its original "Pure Linen" sticker still on it. The poodle seemed to be yearning to break out of the musty linen drawer at last and bring joy to some little girl.

Materials

- Vintage linen tea towel (portrait orientation) for skirt front and back
- 2 embroidered hand towels for skirt side panels
- Luncheon napkin for bodice
- Muslin remnant or another napkin for bodice lining
- Rickrack
- Assorted trim
- Half a handkerchief for straps
- Bodice pattern
- 2 crochet hot pads for pockets

Preparations

Cut the towel across the middle to make two separate panels for the skirt. Turn both panels upright and choose two more linen hand towels for side panels to complement the main feature panels and add fullness to the skirt.

Skirt

Since the vertical panels are finished on both edges, it is not necessary to make a typical seam that would require pressing open. Just overlap side edges of the main panels and the side panels, with their bottom edges lined up, and topstitch through both layers of fabric. Lay the stitched-together skirt on a cutting board and carefully trim the top edge of the skirt so everything is the same length.

Run basting stitches along the top of the skirt and gather it in to fit the bottom of the bodice. Stitch rickrack trim to the bottom edge of the skirt so that it peeks out from under the skirt.

Bodice

Cut out the bodice front and back from a vintage luncheon napkin, making sure you're getting a part of the design that pleases you and that it's located where you want it on each piece. Cut out the lining from another napkin or from scraps of muslin. Sew the side seams of the lining and bodice, then pin the pieces together with wrong sides out. Sew along the top edge, turn right side out, and press. Sew rickrack to the top and bottom edges of the bodice.

Sew the bodice lining and the skirt together. The bottom edge of the bodice, already finished with rickrack, will overhang the skirt.

Embellishment

Cut half a colorful handkerchief in half lengthwise to make two shoulder straps. Fold the two outer edges of each strap toward the center and press. Pin and then topstitch them so they won't unfold. Tie a knot a few inches from the end of each strap, then sew them to the bodice where they best fit your little girl.

Arrange the two colorful hot pads on the side panels for pockets and pin in place. Machine or hand-stitch them in place.

Styling

• For summer, all a girl needs to go with this dress are some sandals and a giant hair bow. For winter, try a nice red long-sleeved T-shirt and some leggings.

Tips

• There are so many beautiful, never-used tea towels out there. Watch for them at estate sales.
• Once you have your center piece, start watching for some solid-color side panels like napkins or tea towels to complete your project.

Blue Bird and Bow Peep

Do you hoard lovely pastel linen guest towels but never use them? Does your grandmother have a stash of fine guest towels just growing old in a linen closet? Step up and give a new life to these beautiful treasures from a different era. It's a design puzzle you'll love putting together and an heirloom that will thrill and delight your child or grandchild. Start collecting the puzzle parts now. The hardest part of this project is collecting the components in the perfect colors to make your heart sing.

Materials

Blue Bird

- 5 linen guest towels
- Special white hand towel for apron
- Handkerchief for second apron and straps
- Small dresser scarf with blue embroidery of a bird
- Scraps of linen for bodice
- Scraps of muslin for bodice lining
- Bodice pattern
- 6 little buttons or silk roses
- Pair of white leggings
- White eyelet ruffle trim

Little Bow Peep

- 5 linen guest towels
- Scraps of linen for bodice
- Scraps of muslin for bodice lining
- Bodice pattern
- Embroidered dresser scarf
- Special linen guest towel for apron
- Small dresser scarf for top apron
- Ribbon
- Rickrack
- Velcro tape
- Pair of white leggings
- End of a linen pillowcase trimmed in tatting or crocheted lace to trim leggings

Skirt

Arrange the five guest towels in a pleasing order. Since none of the towels have raw edges, simply overlap the edges and topstitch along the side seams. Place the shorter apron on top of the slightly longer one, on the center front of the skirt, and pin them both in place. Stitch two rows of basting stitches around the top of the skirt.

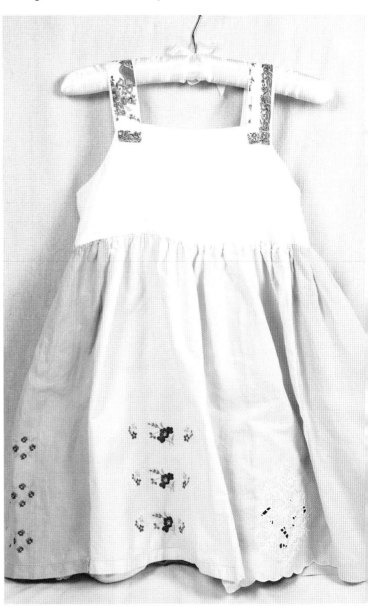

Blue Bird Bodice

Cut out the bodice from a large damask linen napkin, then cut out the lining from soft muslin scraps. Sew the side seams of both parts together and press. With right sides facing, sew the bodice to the bodice lining along the top edge, turn right side out, and press. Press under a ⅝ in. (1.6 cm) seam allowance on the lower edge of the bodice and lining.

Cut half a colorful handkerchief in half lengthwise to make two shoulder straps. Fold the two outer edges of each strap toward the center and press. Pin the straps to the bodice, then topstitch them so they won't unfold. Sew the straps to the bodice where they best fit your little girl.

Pull the basting threads to gather the skirt so that it fits the bodice, pin in place, and sew. Hand-stitch the bodice lining to the inside of the bodice-skirt seam.

Bow Peep Bodice

Cut out the bodice front from one end of an embroidered dresser scarf. Cut out the bodice back from a matching linen scrap. Cut out the bodice lining from soft muslin or linen scraps. Assemble the bodice and lining, following the directions on the pattern. Press. Sew Velcro tape to the sides of the opening in the back of the bodice. Fold under and press a ⅝ in. (1.6 cm) seam allowance around the bottom edge of the bodice and bodice lining. Sew rickrack to the bottom edge of the bodice.

Pull the basting threads to gather the skirt to fit the bodice. Pin the lining of the bodice to the skirt. Sew them together. The finished bottom edge of the bodice will slightly overhang the skirt.

Blue Bird Embellishment

Run a line of basting stitches across the top of the dresser scarf with the blue embroidered bird. Pull the basting threads to gather the scarf so that the scarf fits across the top of the bodice. Pin, then sew it in place. Sew three little buttons or flowers to each corner of the bodice where the straps meet it.

Bow Peep Embellishment

Tie a bow in a length of bright pink ribbon. Pin it to the center of the front of the dress, where the skirt meets the bodice.

Blue Bird Leggings

Sew a length of 1 in. (2.5 cm) eyelet ruffle around the leg openings of a pair of white leggings.

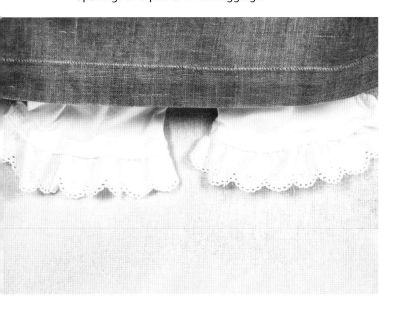

Bow Peep Leggings

Cut off the end of a pillow case with tatting or crochet edging on it, then cut it into two pieces, one for each leg. Sew the two ends of each half together and press the seam. Run basting stitches along the raw edges and pull the threads to gather each piece into a ruffle that fits the leg openings on the leggings. Pin the ruffles in place, then stitch them on the machine. Tie two lengths of hot pink ribbon into bows. Safety pin the bows to the knees of the leggings so they can be removed on laundry day.

Styling

- These dresses bring all that and a bag of chips to the table. Not much more is required. Just add pink ballet slippers or black patent leather Mary Jane shoes and the girls are ready to rock and roll.
- Huge hair bows might be the perfect cherry on the top.
- Leggings or tights and a long-sleeved T-shirt look splendid with the antique linens for cooler weather.

Tips

- These two dresses are perfect for sisters, cousins, or BFFs.
- If you find monogrammed linen hand towels, hoard them for a little girl with that initial.
- A button can easily cover a tiny hole in a vintage linen. Or you can cover a stain or hole with a pretty pocket or a patch made by sewing together a tiny square hankie scrap and a scrap of damask, then turning them right side out.
- Never, ever, ever, ever wash the vintage linens or hankies in the washer or dry them in the dryer. Always wash by hand and hang to dry.

CHAPTER 8

Hankie Panky

That stash of granny's so-cool vintage handkerchiefs is the stuff of which dreamy kid's couture is made. Dig out your favorite hankies and make a fun little frock for your little miss. Fancy Nancy will eat her heart out when she sees your hankie tutu. Or how about wrapping the new baby in a puffy blanket made of grandmother's favorite hankies? Put a little family love in each stitch and use those treasured hankies.

Hankie Blankie

Did your grandmother always carry a freshly laundered and ironed hankie in her pocketbook? Today that tradition has been replaced with paper tissues and some hand sanitizer.

Progress marches on, leaving behind hundreds of graphic treasures too good to toss! Use them to make a hankie blankie for new baby, covered in family memories. Collect a hankie or two from family members and friends, pick up two remnants of colorful fleece, and make a meaningful, useful, colorful gift for any new baby.

Materials

- 5 vintage hankies
- 2 fleece remnants large enough to accommodate the 5 hankies
- Rickrack
- Double-sided lightweight iron-on interfacing (enough to put under the 5 hankies)
- Yardstick
- Chalk
- A dinner plate
- Ribbon roses

Preparations

Hand-launder the hankies and let them air-dry. Press them. Wash and dry the fleece remnants.

Sewing

Lay out one of the fleece pieces on a large table or the floor. Place the five hankies on the fleece and arrange them in a pattern that you like. Take a picture or make notes so you will remember where you are placing them. Following the manufacturer's directions, iron the double-sided interfacing onto the back of each of the hankies, then trim the excess around the edges. Pin the hankies back onto the fleece in the pattern you decided on. Press the hankies onto the fleece, again following the manufacturer's directions. Once they are bonded to the fleece, sew the hankies to the fleece, topstitching about 1/4 in. (6 mm) inside the edge of each hankie.

Lay the fleece out flat again. Use the yardstick and chalk to draw a guide line to stitch down the rickrack around what will become the outside edge of the blanket. Use a dinner plate as a pattern to round the corners. Sew the rickrack right down its center all the way around this line.

Lay the second piece of fleece out faceup, then lay the embellished fleece top facedown on top of it—making them right side to right side. Pin the two pieces together. Follow the line of stitching from the rickrack on the back of the embellished top as you sew the two pieces of fleece together. Leave an opening about 4 in. (10 cm) long to turn the blankie. Trim the edges, leaving a 1/2 in. (1.3 cm) seam allowance, then turn the blanket right side out. Sew the opening shut and press the blanket carefully on a low setting with a damp cloth between the iron and the blanket. Topstitch around the quilt about 1 in. (2.5 cm) in from the outside edge. Securely tack down ribbon roses in the centers of the hankies and in the blank spots to hold the top and bottom of the quilt together.

Tips

- Solicit hankies from family members to make special memories in the quilt.
- A quilt like this would be perfect to keep at grandmother's house for baby to play on.
- You can make a more "manly" version with bright red, blue, green, yellow, and brown hankies.

Hankie Top and Tablecloth Skirt

Simply sweet—that is what you call a top made from two pretty little vintage hankies. Want to give a new baby in your family something with sentimental value, but don't have a big budget? Want to give something that is upcycled but has family memories included? This is your project! If you are feeling confident, add a round tablecloth skirt to the mix and you have a completely green outfit for your little sweetie. Since they are not so hot in current decorating trends, it is easy to find a really nice little round tablecloth for not a lot of money at estate sales and thrift shops. Better still, bet a relative has one and would be happy to donate it for the enhancement of Little Bit's wardrobe.

Materials

Hankie Top

- 2 coordinating hankies of the same size
- Four 18 in. (46 cm) strips of ribbon 1 in. (2.5 cm) wide
- 1 yd. (0.9 m) bias tape, $7/8$ in. (2.2 cm) wide

Tablecloth Skirt

- Round tablecloth
- String
- Chalk
- Elastic, $7/8$ or 1 in. (2.2 or 2.5 cm) wide
- Roll of tulle, 6 in. (15 cm) wide

Preparation

Hand-wash two coordinating handkerchiefs and press them. Hand-wash the tablecloth and soak in stain remover if badly stained. If you can't get any spots out that way, choose a nice button, bow, or appliqué to place over the troublesome spot later. Air-dry the tablecloth and then press it.

Top

Lay out the two hankies and fold under the top two corners of each. This will form the underarm section of the top. Pin the bias tape to the inside top edge of each hankie, then sew it in place along the top edge. Trim the hankie edge under the tape, then pin the lower edge of the bias tape in place and stitch it down.

Slightly overlap the side seams of the two hankies and topstitch both side seams. Sewing the seams in this manner saves you from having a seam to press open and keeps the top as wide as it can be.

Embellishment

Fold under and press one end of each of the four ribbons for the straps. Sew the folded end of two ribbons on the inside front and two on the inside back to form the shoulder straps. Try the top on the child and tie the straps at the shoulders in bows.

the elastic fits in one of the four sections of the circle. Fold under the elastic circle, pin in place, and stitch again to attach the other edge of the waistband to the skirt. You now have a circle skirt with an elastic waistband.

Embellishment

Sew a tulle ruffle to the inside bottom edge of the skirt where the decorative crochet lace meets the tablecloth, pushing little tucks of tulle under the presser foot as you sew the tulle to the skirt. This will make a nice under-skirt ruffle.

Styling

- This carefree summer ensemble just needs some flip-flops or sandals to make a family heritage statement.
- The top is precious with the tablecloth skirt, but it would be equally at home with a pair of jeans, a jeans skirt, or a little ruffled three-tier skirt or shorts.

Tips

- This is such a sentimental upcycled gift. A couple of handkerchiefs from a family connection is all it takes. Using Great-Aunt Betty's hankies, you could sew up a little top in no time at all. It would make the perfect gift for a new baby in the family. The gift is upcycled, doesn't cost a penny, and yet demonstrates the continuity of family love.
- If your two hankies are not wide enough for the top, add a pretty lace panel down each side to increase the width.
- Don't toss a beautifully worked tablecloth just because there is a grape jelly stain that won't go away. A big button or a little appliqué patch can cover a little oops.

Skirt

Measure the child's waist. Subtract about 2 in. (5 cm) from that measurement and cut a string that length. Place the string in a circle in the center of the tablecloth. Trace the circle in chalk on the tablecloth.

Cut a strip of elastic the same length as the string. Overlap the two ends of the elastic about 1 in. (2.5 cm) and sew them together. Make four marks on your elastic, evenly spaced, to divide it into fourths. Using chalk, mark the circle you drew on the tablecloth to divide it into four equal sections. Carefully cut the circle out of the tablecloth, then pin the elastic circle around the circle cut in the tablecloth, using your marks for reference. Use the sewing machine to sew the elastic to the right side of the skirt along the edge of the circle, stretching it just enough that each quarter of

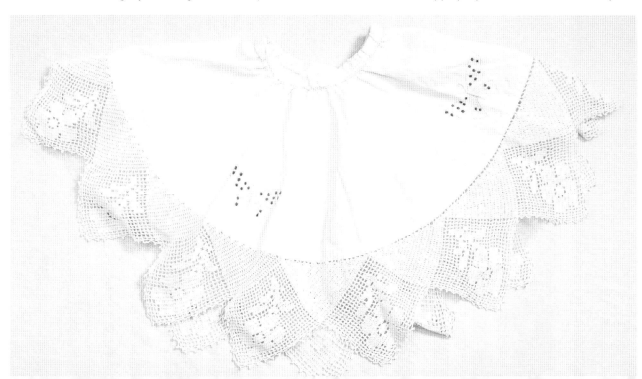

Hankie Tutus

The graphics, embellishments, and colors on vintage handkerchiefs are all irresistible! Use your great-auntie's hankie collection or find inexpensive hankies at estate sales. Hankies bring a whole lot of perky color and punch to a girl's wardrobe for such a little expenditure. Hankie tutus make the best shower gifts you can imagine. Paired with a matching onesie and tucked into a glory of tissue paper, they are shower show-stoppers! The hankie tutu also works as a charming skirt over shorts or leggings for a toddler or young girl.

Materials

- 5 hankies, plus 1 more for an apron if you wish
- Elastic for waistband
- Ribbon for a bow
- Safety pin
- Cotton bias tape, rayon bias tape, or lace for waistband casing

Preparations

Choose five hankies that, placed together, make your heart sing. Hand-wash the hankies and air-dry them flat on towels. Do not put the hankies in the washer or dryer.

Decide if you want the bottom hem of the tutu to be even or helter-skelter. All hankies are not the same size. A little variation in the hemline won't make a big difference but it makes life easier if the five hankies are approximately the same size.

Decide which of the five hankies you want to be the center feature of your tutu. It is usually the bell-ringer, the most smashing of all the handkerchiefs. Sometimes I choose a pretty, plain, solid-colored hankie and use another smaller hankie over the center one as an apron. As the designer, you make the call.

Once you have chosen your center front panel (hankie or hankie plus smaller apron hankie) then decide on the placement of the other four hankies. The seam of two hankies will be the center back of your tutu. Two others will flank the center panel. When you have the order of placement of the five panels, proceed with one of the methods below, depending on what kind of hem you want.

Method 1: Random Hem Length

This is the easiest method. Pin the five hankies together in the order you have chosen, starting by pinning the center panel to the hankies on either side. Overlap the edges of the hankies, putting the one with the prettier edge on top of the other.

Top stitch over the overlapped area to sew those three panels together, then pin and stitch the last two panels to the sides of the right and left center panels.

Method 2: Even Hem Length

Lay your five hankies out in order in a row, lining up the bottom edges. Fold over the tops of the hankies so that they all match the height of your shortest hankie. Pin the folded-over top of each of the taller ones to itself. Those edges will be stitched down when the waistband casing is sewn in place. Pin the right and left front panels to the main center panel, overlapping the edges with the prettier edge on the top. Topstitch these seams. Now pin the two back panels to the front and side panels and stitch.

Apron

If you have chosen to add a smaller hankie to serve as the apron, now is the time to sew it down. Center the apron hankie on top of the center hankie, with the top edges lined up. Pin the apron hankie down, then sew it in place along the top edge.

Waistband

Pin the bias tape to the wrong side of the top edge of the skirt, about ½ in. (1.3 cm) below the edge. Sew the bias tape in place along both edges, leaving an opening on one edge to thread the elastic through.

Measure the little girl's tummy and cut the elastic about an inch smaller. For shower gifts and tutus for newborns, I make skirts with a 16 in. (41 cm) waist that can be expanded later as the child grows. Pin a safety pin to the end of the elastic, and use it to thread the elastic through the casing. Overlap the ends about 1 in. (2.5 cm). Try the skirt on the little girl, if possible, to check the fit, then sew the two overlapping ends of the elastic together. Sew the opening in the casing closed.

Embellishment

Choose a pretty ribbon from the scrap bag that goes well with your design. Tie it in a perky bow. Use a safety pin to pin the bow at the center front of the waistband, so that it can be removed to wash the tutu.

Styling

- This project makes a great gift for a new baby girl.
- This tutu over a onesie makes a big fashion statement for a little girl!
- Older girls can wear theirs over bathing suits, shorts, jeans, or leggings.

Tips

- This is such a sentimental project. Get a hankie from each grandmother and great-grandmother and make an ivory hankie tutu for the baby girl's christening.
- These hankies are fragile; do not wash or dry them in any machine! Hand-wash and let them air-dry.
- Carry one of these in your diaper bag so your little one will always have a cute outfit at hand.
- Sew up a batch of these and have them ready for friends and relatives who have new baby girls.

IVORY VARIATION ✳ This variation uses five same-size ivory hankies with one smaller one for the apron. All of these hankies have tatting or lace on their four edges. In order to maximize that beautiful lace, the seams on this tutu are sewn on the outside, instead of by overlapping the edges so one is on the inside. That allows each seam to feature two different lace edges. Sew the bias tape for the waistband to the inside of the skirt about 1 in. (2.5 cm) below the top edge, so that the lace edges of the top of the hankies will form a lacy ruffle around the waist. Cap this one off with a pretty ivory bow front and center.

Acknowledgments

Many thanks to phenomenal editors Deb Smith and Kathryn Fulton and to Stackpole Books for this opportunity to help save the earth. Heartfelt thanks to my friends and family, especially Trinity, who graciously enabled me to do this project by supplying me with upcycled treasures and brilliant ideas and by serving as mannequins and life coaches. You are blessings in my life.